EMERSON IN ITALY

EMERSON IN ITALY

PHOTOGRAPHS BY
EVELYN HOFER

TEXT BY
EVELYN BARISH

HENRY HOLT AND COMPANY
NEW YORK

Published by Henry Holt and Company, Inc.,
115 West 18th Street, New York, New York 10011.
Published in Canada by Fitzhenry & Whiteside Limited,
195 Allstate Parkway, Markham, Ontario L3R 4T8.

Library of Congress Cataloging-in-Publication Data
Emerson in Italy.
Includes bibliographical references.
1. Emerson, Ralph Waldo, 1803–1882—Journeys—Italy.
2. Authors, American—19th century—Biography.
3. Italy—Description and travel—1801–1860.   I. Hofer,
Evelyn.   II. Barish, Evelyn.   III. Emerson, Ralph
Waldo, 1803–1882.
PS1634.E44   1989   814'.3   88-8326
ISBN 0-8050-0914-0

Henry Holt books are available at special discounts
for bulk purchases for sales promotions, premiums,
fund-raising, or educational use. Special editions
or book excerpts can also be created to specification.

  For details, contact:

Special Sales Director
Henry Holt and Company, Inc.
115 West 18th Street
New York, New York 10011

First Edition

Designed by Lucy Albanese
Printed in Italy
10 9 8 7 6 5 4 3 2 1

TO CELESTE BARTOS

ACKNOWLEDGMENTS

I wish to thank Andreas Pauly, who assisted me in this project. In the Italy of *1986–87* I hoped to convey the timelessness of that country which Emerson saw in *1833*. Without the sensitivity and patience of Andreas, I would not have been able to realize my desire.

I am grateful also to all the Italian people who helped me in their museums and institutions when I encountered adversity.

Evelyn Hofer

Many people have assisted me and have my thanks, but I am particularly indebted to Paul Mitarachi and Barbara Plant. He helped me to begin, she to prevail.

The Pinewood Foundation supported the project with far more than institutional loyalty; Evelyn Hofer and I owe it a unique debt. At an earlier stage I received welcome support from the PSC-CUNY Research Awards Program.

I acknowledge with thanks the permission of the Ralph Waldo Emerson Memorial Association and the Houghton Library to quote from the *Journals and Miscellaneous Notebooks of Ralph Waldo Emerson* and from *The Letters of Ralph Waldo Emerson.*

Evelyn Barish
New York City, May 1988

EMERSON: LANGUAGE AND BACKGROUND

The main source of Emerson's language in this narrative is volume 4 of the *Journals and Miscellaneous Notebooks of Ralph Waldo Emerson*, ed. Alfred Ferguson et al., 16 vols. (Cambridge, Mass.: Harvard University Press, 1960–1982). Letters when quoted come from volume 1 of *The Letters of Ralph Waldo Emerson*, ed. Ralph L. Rusk, 6 vols. (New York: Columbia University Press, 1939), and are cited in the text by date. References to Emerson's essays and poems come from *The Complete Works of Ralph Waldo Emerson*, ed. Edward W. Emerson, 12 vols. (Cambridge, Mass.: Riverside Press, 1904), and are identified in the text by title. For a more extensive, scholarly discussion of this era in his life, see my critical biography, *Emerson: The Roots of Prophecy* (Princeton University Press, forthcoming in 1989), and—for more general information—the "Selected Sources" listed at the end of this text.

EMERSON IN ITALY

THE UPSTART

"Here we come & mean to be welcome."

ON Christmas Day, *1832*, Ralph Waldo Emerson watched Boston Harbor quickly recede in the winter gale that was carrying him and his ship to Europe. Some weeks earlier, he had gone to book passage for Puerto Rico and join his brother Edward for a few warm winter months. Instead, he had come back with "purpureal visions," as he wrote his brother William, of spending half a year in Italy. Within days a different ticket was in hand, and now he was actually embarked on the brig *Jasper* for Malta, Sicily, Italy, and points north. If he was acting on impulse, it obviously had come from a very deep level.* During the next nine months of his journey he would explore that prompting until he was ready to come back a changed man, able to use it creatively.

In a few years the renegade minister would publish *Nature* and with that make himself America's most liberating voice, but as he stood at the rail Emerson, then twenty-nine, had a great deal to think about—and a great deal gladly to leave behind. To those around him he must have seemed a rather striking figure: six feet tall, thin, and a bit gangly, with brown hair and eyes of an intense, penetrating blue. His voice was rich and had a peculiar and courtly hesitation in it as he searched for precisely the right word. Deep intelligence and perception showed in his eyes and mouth, determination and perhaps some sadness appeared in the set of his mouth and square chin. The grand beak of his nose came from his mother's side of the family.

He had every reason to feel successful. He had been foremost among all the candidates for ordination in his generation, and congregations had competed for him before he had accepted the prize of the prestigious Second Church. His wife,

*See "Emerson: Language and Background," on page vii, for the sources of quotations from Emerson and facts about his life.

Ellen Tucker Emerson, had been an heiress, her family glad to admit him to their circle, for the Emerson name and his own talents brought cachet to their solid bourgeois world.

But troubles lay heavy on him. Some came from grief over Ellen's early death. She was gone almost two years now, but she had been "the romance of [his] life." Her loss had moved him almost beyond any other, and it haunted him still. The other troubles were professional, intellectual, and religious. He was a minister, but on grounds of conscience he had renounced his pulpit four months earlier. He could not continue to offer one of Christianity's central sacraments, he had told his congregation. Serving Communion—symbolically eating the flesh and drinking the blood of Christ—no longer seemed to him a holy but rather a pagan rite, viscerally repugnant and foreign, not a matter of faith.

Emerson was a Unitarian, ordained in the rationalistic branch of Congregationalism that dominated the circles of power in New England's capital. In spite of the Revolution, America was far from being an egalitarian democracy as we know it, and Waldo Emerson (he had dropped the Ralph in adolescence) was the sixth generation of his family to be a minister and the quintessential New England "aristocrat," as the term was commonly used, to mean an élite class. In Boston, whose first Puritan governor, John Winthrop, had also been its first minister and financial mainstay, the clergy had always been leaders, and such descent gave Emerson entrée to the city's inner circle.

It would have been easy for him to remain in his pulpit, keep his doubts to himself, and lead the life of a privileged man in a time of great national growth. Many did, and none criticized. But Emerson could not, for he was marked by scrupulous integrity and was an original and iconoclastic thinker keenly aware that he lived in a new era. A great upheaval was sweeping Western thought and politics, changing national borders, and creating free men and women out of serfs and peasants. It was the Romantic age, when art, social customs, and beliefs about human nature were under question. In Europe, the French Revolution followed by Napoleon's wars had changed society; in America, the Federal period was giving way to the Age of Jackson and the coming of the age of the common man.

America was on the brink of great change, but it did not know it yet. Emerson knew it, and he wanted to be one of its prophets. "The seer," he wrote, "is always the sayer." Abolition loomed on the horizon; women's rights were about to be debated. Important as these issues were, Emerson was concerned even more with creating the underlying conditions, the intellectual freedom in which they could be argued. Among advanced thinkers, critical thought was now valued and old assumptions were questioned. The Enlightenment in the eighteenth century had made history a method of analysis, not a mere recounting of old narratives and legends. Scientists, especially geologists, were making discoveries that threatened the Bible's teachings, and its history and miracles now seemed flimsy and inadequate.

Finding one's way was difficult. New faiths were springing up everywhere. It was a time of agonizing struggle for persons who respected both their faith and their intellect. When Emerson wrote in "Life and Letters in New England" that "the young men were born with knives in their brain," he was describing his own youthful self.

More than that was involved, however, for the traveler. For despite his heritage, his family had been poor, and he had lived in but not of his society. More important, he was temperamentally and intellectually a rebel, a nonconformist. "I like the sayers of Nay better than the sayers of Yea," he wrote.

HIS parishioners at the Second Church (literally the second oldest church in New England), however, were conventional men and women. They were sympathetic with their young leader, many sided with him, and there was good will on both sides, but inevitably the majority voted to accept the resignation he had offered. Now he was on the high seas with no job, only a little money, and the great unresolved question of how and where to speak his mind. His wife had left him an inheritance, and he was able to live on its small income as long as he stayed single.

Moreover, a physical enemy had attacked him: his old, "indolent" case of tuberculosis had returned. This was a horrifying illness that had ravaged his family, killing Ellen and his oldest brother, and contributing to the early death of his father. Soon it was to carry off two more of his three surviving brothers. When he departed he was, as he wrote his aunt in April *1833*, "a wasted peevish invalid." To an impartial observer, Captain Ellis of the *Jasper*, he seemed unlikely to survive the voyage.

His disease was the scourge of its age. No one knew what caused consumption; only quacks pretended to cure it. TB could show up almost anywhere in the body, and, beginning in his early twenties, it had made inroads first in his eyes, then in his joints, and finally in his lungs. At twenty-three he had already been forced on one lifesaving journey south for his health, and before that he had undergone two experimental but useless operations on his eyes to relieve the dimness of sight and pressure behind the cornea caused by the infection.

Long before medicine became a science, however, Emerson—like others who survived consumption—became his own doctor, learning to recognize its symptoms and manage his illness with unflagging patience, discipline, and strategy. When the "mouse in [his] chest" grew troublesome, he had learned to leave his desk and find relief from stress with laughing companions; when his hip or knee grew lame from the inflammation that TB caused in the joints, he knew exactly how long he must walk to keep up strength and mobility before reaching what he called in a letter of February *1828* "the end of the rope of my rheumatism."

Consumption was highly responsive to stress: fatigue, grief, anxiety—all could trigger attacks. Warm weather, a sea voyage, rest, and separation from the causes of worry were the prescriptions of choice. Emerson knew this, and he knew too that months of diarrhea, a common symptom of his form of the illness, had left him weak and probably dangerously underweight. It was time to get away and make himself well.

BUT he had even deeper reasons for making this voyage. For this was a spiritual journey on which he aimed consciously to achieve what he called "the Anointed eye"—that is, a vision open to the universe and its grace. He wanted nothing less than to change his life and himself, to feel "the growth of his true self." He wanted, as he was to write in *Nature*, "an original relation with the universe."

These were high ambitions, but Emerson knew he had talents to match them. This knowledge, however, was at odds with his sense of identity. There was a discrepancy between his accomplished public self and what he privately felt himself to be. Appearances to the contrary, he was often ill at ease. A fatherless and impoverished childhood had meant that he had begun earning his living at fourteen by teaching—doing so at the same time he had entered Harvard.

He grew up without much attention in a household burdened by debt and illness, dependent at times for their very survival on charity. To feed her five sons, his mother kept a boardinghouse, and all the boys worked. Waldo gave his energies to work and private dreams, and kept his talents to himself. He called his youth "unpromising," though a few in the family perceived his extraordinary talents. When he competed for prizes in college, he came in second, probably because his ideas were too original and risky for his Harvard professors, central members of the Establishment.

4

After graduating at eighteen, Emerson kept school, sent his two younger brothers through college, helped the older one go to Europe for further study, suffered the first breakdown of his health—and managed, through it all, to get his precious license to preach as a minister. Eager always to help his mother and brothers financially, he sacrificed himself and missed a great deal of the social experiences that other boys took for granted.

His marriage at age twenty-six to a beautiful young heiress and his appointment at the Second Church had been the first public signs that the world was taking notice of his abilities. By then his character and manner had grown firm and clear. From living and from sickness, he had learned patience to accompany his insight. But he had learned more: he knew that he had not yet finished growing. And he knew in particular that there was no such thing for him as "easy live and quiet die." Risk was part of life; death could come for anyone, as it had stalked all whom he had loved best. Better to follow his visions, however "purple," than not to try.

America was still colonial in spirit, if not in fact, and no new national thinker had arisen to put into accessible, popular language the ideas of independence and intellectual freedom that had guided Jefferson and Franklin and the framers of the Constitution. The country's best-known writer, Washington Irving, for example, now spent his time traveling abroad, writing up his tourism. His advice to Americans back home was to study Europe as a great "Golden book" in order to avoid its mistakes and perhaps one day aim at its glories.

Emerson understood how sterile that path—and all imitation—would be. Instead he wanted to show his country his vision of a culture that would be open to the young, the autonomous, the creative. He hated the tyranny of timid minds; he scorned acts motivated by fear of criticism, carried out in hypocrisy. He wanted to express a creed that found God and ethics not in books, traditions, or church history, but in human beings engaged in action.

He was a child of Romanticism, fired by the great Romantic belief in the future: "Who can set bounds to the possibilities of man?" he was to ask. He had named the journal he kept from age sixteen "The Wide World," but the narrow sphere of his youth he later called "the corpse-cold Unitarianism of Brattle Street" and Harvard College. It preached respect for the past and already practiced the almost Chinese ancestor-worship that came to be associated with the "Boston Brahmins." Emerson wanted to make a world more free.

To do that, however, he must first free himself. In *1832*, though he had been preaching for years, he still felt tongue-tied: "The presence of other people . . . embarrasses [him]," he wrote in his journal. "The reason is, himself is a peppercorn & his relations to other people are the whole world in his imagination. The only remedy must be from the growth of his true self."

In embarking for Europe, he was engaging with what his friend Clough would call the "land of Empire, Art, and Love"—the Old World of high culture and corruption, source of richness and anxiety to all Americans. Paradoxically, the man who was to insist that Americans see themselves as "central men," not secondary or provincial, who was to tell America how to get beyond the ingrained, ducking habits of its colonial past, was going from the New World to the Old World to renew his life, if not to save it. But though much was uncertain, one thing was clear: the journey would test his ambitions. If he grew more ill, if the work of travel fatigued rather than inspired him, if he met no useful persons—if any of a hundred mischances occurred—it would be worse than a waste. If it succeeded, the future would have a very wide horizon.

"WHAT is a passenger?" Emerson asked while traveling:

> He is a much enduring man who bends under the load of his leisure. He fawns upon the Captain, reveres the mate, but his eye follows the Steward; scans accurately as symptomatic, all the motions of that respectable officer.
>
> The species is contemplative, given to imitation, viciously inquisitive, immensely capable of sleep, large eaters, swift digesters, their thoughts ever running on men & things ashore & their eye usually squinting over the bulwark, to estimate the speed of the bubbles.

The worst was behind him when he wrote this, but as his cheerful tone suggests, sea voyages made Emerson feel better almost at once. The crossing took almost seven weeks, and for a week he and the other passengers were confined to their cabins: "Nausea, darkness, unrest, uncleanness, harpy appetite & harpy feeding, the ugly sound of water in mine ears, anticipations of going to the bottom, & the treasures of memory" occupied his mind.

But though unshaven after ten days, "a grinning Esau," he proved an excellent traveler, flexible and forbearing. The family's heroic motto had been his Aunt Mary's command, "Scorn trifles," and he applied this to his position where "in a cabin . . . people become all eye." It was "a great part of wellbeing to ignorize a good deal" about one's fellowman and not notice his warts "or expect the hour when he shall wash his teeth." His fellow passengers were four: a couple named S. P. Holbrook and their daughter Miss E., and Samuel Kettell. Holbrook and Kettell had done some hack writing for the publisher Samuel Griswold Goodrich. Emerson did not care for these people, but he scrupulously avoided any comment until long out of their company.

After two weeks of wet decks, thudding seas, noises everywhere, and not more than an hour of sunshine at a time, his health had actually improved, and he boasted of "a truckman's health & stomach." The winds though rough were warm. Soon he dispensed with his overcoat, and his underlying good humor rose to the surface.

> We have sauntered all this calm day at one or two knots the hour and nobody on board well pleased but I. And why should I be pleased? I have nothing to record. I have read little. I have done nothing. . . . I will be pleased though I do not deserve it.

He was beginning to believe he deserved his place in the sun. He credited his recuperation to "celestial gifts." But heavenly help at sea—as Napoleon said of war—came to the soul with the strongest artillery, and Emerson's weapon against disease was the clarity of his hopes and purposes. He found ways to think and be alone: "I rose at sunrise and under the lee of the spencer sheet had a solitary thoughtful hour. All right thought is devout."

Humor was another defense. When he could not leave his berth, he had amused himself by "remember[ing] up nearly the whole of Lycidas, clause by clause, here a verse & there a word." Milton's long poem eulogized a young clergyman drowned at sea—and contained his famous attack on the venal self-interest of the established clergy: "The hungry sheep look up and are not fed."

The long voyage gave him time to observe the dangerous calling of the sea: " 'A prison with the chance of being drowned.' " He admired the practical intelligence of the captain and crew. When the sailors unquestioningly risked their lives to execute an order, or the captain showed he could bleed a sick man, catch a porpoise to make oil from its blubber and steak from its meat, and with only a quadrant and chart "find his way across *3000* miles of stormy water into a little gut of inland sea with as much precision as if led by a clue," Emerson thought him "worth a thousand philosophers." He had an intellectual's respect for men of action and the grace to acknowledge their gifts.

But he was haunted by recurring doubts. Only a few years later, he was to write in "Self-Reliance" that "envy is ignorance; . . . imitation is suicide," but now he felt himself less competent, and the journey he was undertaking must have had a threatening side. He had never been out of America before, nor spoken a foreign language. (Italian and German he was teaching himself.) He had no friends abroad, and no introductions to eminent men. He would have to find entrée to persons of intellectual merit as he went along.

From that perspective, he felt like a juvenile approaching a crotchety old man. "Peeps up Old Europe? . . . hospitably[?] Nay, the slumberous old giant cannot bestir himself in these his chair days." Europe would not bother to amuse "his upstart grandchildren as they come shoal after shoal to salute their old Progenitor, the old Adam of all." For imaginary indifference, he returned imaginary impertinence. "Sleep on, old Sire . . ." Americans would peek and pry "into your towns & towers & keeping-rooms. Here we come & mean to be welcome. So be good now, clever old gentleman."

The cheeky adolescent swagger, pushing old Europe back into its fireside chair, covered anxiety and discontent with himself. What lay ahead? It was not physical danger Emerson dwelt on—in all his writings there is no hint that this mattered much to him. But would he prove equal to the experience itself? The sailors' prompt obedience amazed him because he had himself always "wondered at" authority, and "thin skins do not believe in thick."

To speak with authority he would need an affirming voice, but he knew that "the thing set down in words is not affirmed. It must affirm itself or no forms of grammar . . . can give it evidence." It was not the writing of an idea that mattered; it was the capacity, so to speak, to live inside it, so that its truth and expression would be natural and inevitable. He knew he had a writer's gift, yet "we but half express ourselves, but ever draw diagonals between our own thought & the supposed thought of our companion & so fail to satisfy either." Going straight to the mark was his aim.

Part of his sense of being challenged came from knowing that Europe was "the place of History." He might put it down as "Lilliput" and the "ant hill of your genealogy," but it could not be argued away. For years Emerson had studied history, hoping to find that humanity's story proved religion's truth. But he had come away disgusted rather than inspired by what it told; the evidence for God's purpose would have to lie elsewhere.

Still, if history was a cheat, it had left wonderful records of its play across Europe, and especially in Italy, first colonized by the Greeks, shaped by the Romans, birth-place of the Renaissance. How could he, so green, a sprat among "shoals" of return-ing "spawn" get from this "place of History" what he needed? Like Goethe before him, another northerner who went south for a life-changing Italian journey, he both expected and needed to learn a great deal about how to live.

EMERSON needed the cocky spirit and good health the long passage gave him. The Grand Tour—for that was what he was embarking on—was both a well-defined route and a demanding one. Three of his heroes had taken it—Montaigne, Goethe, and Byron—and written books about their voyages. Emerson traveled with Goethe in his valise and Byron (perhaps less a hero than a weakness for the American minister) in his heart. *Childe Harold*, the English lord's epic poem about his unhappy hero's journey throughout the Mediterranean, fired the imagination of generations of readers. Adventure, lyricism, and music characterized Byron's immensely popular poetry, but his lasting influence probably came from his passionate concern for freedom and his capacity for indignation. In a Europe still largely ruled by repressive courts, Byron's rebelliousness was as infectious as his zest for life. He had died a hero's death only eight years earlier, fighting with the Greeks for their liberty at Missolonghi.

As for Montaigne, that famous sixteenth-century skeptic important to Emerson had formulated over two centuries earlier what many modern thinkers took as an axiom. In his "Apology for Raymond Seybond" he found useless the airy, empty reasonings of philosophy not tied to empirical fact. "What do I know?" the Frenchman had asked. "He who understands nothing about himself, what can he understand?" The primary facts must be found in one's own experience. He would root his understanding of things in self-study. He had traveled abroad especially in Italy, seeking both health and the grasp of real life that flowed from adapting to the customs of the people around him and mingling with them, humble and great. Emerson quoted him at the beginning of his journey: "Wherever we go, self is the sole subject we study & learn. Montaigne said, himself was all he knew. Myself is much more than I know & yet I know nothing else."

The great German poet Goethe had also pursued the same aim. At a time of crisis in his thirties, when he was already well known as a writer and successful as a public man but frustrated as a creative artist, Goethe had literally fled by night with no servants, carrying only a valise and some manuscripts, escaping from the small duchy he helped govern, telling no one of his plans and not writing until he was safely across the Alps in the land "where the lemon trees bloom," which he had longed for years to see. To him it represented not only freedom and the birthplace of art, but also a land where he could remake himself, learn his true faults and virtues, and find a way to complete the many plays and poems he had begun but not brought to solid life. He aimed to study nature closely, and to come back "reborn," knowing better how to live and how to work—less frantically, less compulsively, more coherently. His fame was worldwide by the time his travel journal was published.

Goethe was still alive when Emerson traveled. The young American took the *Italian Journey* along with him in the original version partly to improve his German, but far more (since he did not plan to visit that country) for the inspiration of its example.

The itinerary that all such travelers followed, intellectual giants and ordinary people alike, was well delineated, as Paul Baker has shown.* In the south, it stressed Sicily, the remains of the great Greek colonies at Syracuse and elsewhere, a visit to Etna, and calls at Messina, Palermo, and Catania. The *mezzogiorno*—mainland Italy south of Naples—was ignored, as it tends to be even today. Naples, also founded by the Greeks, was for many still the greatest attraction of all. *"Vedi Napoli e poi mori"* was the common assertion: See Naples and die.

Then came Rome, where travelers seldom stayed less than a month, a journey through the hill towns to Florence, which absorbed another month, and a leg northeast through Bologna and Ferrara to Venice and its neighboring cities of Verona and Vicenza. Then, out through the Brenner pass to Germany, or west along the Po Valley to Milan, and through the Alps to Switzerland. In the days of sails and horse-drawn carriages, when visitors engaged in active study and visited both the places and the people of interest repeatedly, such a journey might easily take a year.

Reaching those great cities involved real dangers and many discomforts. Travel by sea was often quicker and safer than a shorter overland route, and to get from the eastern to the western end of Sicily, or from Palermo to Naples, one boarded a *felucca*, a little vessel manned by a small, informally organized crew. With good winds and an absence of pirates, it could cross the Tyrrhenian Sea in two or three days. On land, most long-distance travelers hired a *vettura*, a coach usually owned by its driver who for a flat sum customarily undertook to provide meals and lodging en route. Where the mountains in rocky Italy came down to the sea, or rushing rivers made bridges impossible, the coach might have to roll along the beach itself, skirting the waves, or be unhitched from its horses and ferried across.

Bad as the roads were, they were often better than the inns. A small shelf of travel books had sprung up by the early 1830s, and their lists of necessities for the trip amount virtually to a traveling household. Among the more exotic items were leather sheets, which could be filled with straw—itself frequently too dirty to be used alone—and would be proof against vermin. (Goethe's friend Hackert loaned him a leather mattress, which proved most useful.) In Montaigne's day, foreigners were surprised to find windows without glass or sashes, only heavy wooden shutters, good merely for shutting out storms; in the late eighteenth century these still existed. Sometimes there was no inn at all, with or without windows, and private homes had to be sought, or lodging found in a stable.

10

Travelers complained less of the coaches than the coachmen and porters, who might turn out to be devoted and resourceful, or unreliable and corrupt, in cahoots with vendors to supply inferior goods. Italy was composed of many distinct kingdoms

*Paul R. Baker, *The Fortunate Pilgrims: Americans in Italy 1800–1860* (Cambridge, Mass.: Harvard University Press, 1964), chapter 3.

and duchies, none truly independent of the hostile French and Austrians, who had carved up the great peninsula and its islands; this added to the sense of anarchy. The currency changed at every border, and passports—not always easy to get—were required. Bribes were often expected. In the south, especially in Sicily, the great princes kept private armies to ensure their own and their guests' free passage through their lands, for bandits abounded. The roots of the Mafia are evident in the tale of the intrepid but indignant woman traveler Mariana Starke, who accepted the protection of the Prince of Biscari's soldiers when she crossed southern Sicily, but discovered that these men were only *banditi* on retainer, as it were—and lecherous to boot. Starke and her two noblewomen companions especially objected, as she related in her very popular *Travels in Europe: For the Use of Travellers on the Continent [and] Sicily*, when, on descending from the coach at a rushing stream, she had to step down onto the knee of a demonstrative guard.

One of the most irritating obstacles was quarantine, which any state might impose at its borders, though few did. Within Italy proper, disease was associated with low-lying lands, and because malaria was endemic, many refused to travel at all across the depopulated Campagna, the area surrounding Rome and the basin of the Tiber, during the wrong season. The Pontine marshes, lying between Naples and Rome, were also seen as the haunt of criminals and disease, and coaches hurried across.

But the rewards more than repaid the effort. The country itself was gorgeous, the people for the most part natural and kind, and the southern climate gave to flowers and all growing things colors and richness far greater than visitors from the north had known before. Naples, Palermo, and Catania were situated on famous bays, and if mountains did not rise up behind an Italian town, it might perch itself directly on a peak, ready to spy out approaching strangers, offering cooling fountains and imposing cathedrals carved from the local rock. Montaigne noticed early that the Italians had mastered the craft of terracing, less practiced in the north, and surrounded their fairy-tale peaks with circles of wheat, bordered by rims of vineyards.

Olive and lemon trees were known to northerners only from the schoolroom, and to see them—icons as much as plants—actually growing moved Shelley, for one, to high excitement when he came to the coast north of Naples: "On one side precipitous mountains, whose bases slope into an inclined plane of olive and orange copses, the latter forming . . . an emerald sky of leaves, starred with innumerable globes of their ripening fruit; on the other, the sea. . . ."*

Abundant life and a good climate prevailed all over the Mediterranean, however.

*The Letters of Percy Bysshe Shelley, ed. Frederick L. Jones, 2 vols. (Oxford: Clarendon Press, 1964), 2:83.

What made Italy unique was its combination of art, classical architecture, and the history of Western culture associated with these structures. The artistic tradition was so intense and long that in the late eighteenth century Goethe's journal reported that classical works were still being discovered and brought to living artists like Angelica Kauffmann for authentication and sale, just as workmen had brought the *Apollo Belvedere* to Michelangelo three hundred years before when they had unearthed it in a garden.

In the *1780s*, the Englishman Patrick Brydone climbed all night to the top of Etna to see the sun rise from a horizon he calculated to be two thousand miles in circumference; then he had looked down into the volcano's maw:

> We arrived in full time to see the most wonderful and most sublime sight in Nature . . . a tremendous gulph so celebrated in all ages. . . . The most enthusiastic imagination in the midst of all its terrors, hardly ever formed an idea of a hell more dreadful. It was with a mixture of both pleasure and pain that we quitted this awful scene.

His delighted eighteenth-century description of this example of the horrible sublime inspired other travelers when it appeared in his book *A Tour Through Sicily & Malta*. Vesuvius, looming over Naples, produced similar delicious *frissons*. But when Goethe—mindful of Brydone's feat but less fortunate in his timing—climbed it and got too close, he got a shower of hot pellets, a lungful of vile smoke, and a good scare for his pains.

Certain works of art, like the volcanoes, had become icons, or essential symbols of the Italian experience, and every wayfarer expected to see them—the so-called *Dying Gladiator*, the Medici *Venus*, the head of the *Medusa* in the Rondanini Palace, and innumerable others. (Mrs. Starke seems to have begun the practice of codifying the degree of awe and attention each deserved by awarding exclamation points to these works—one to five, like the newspapers' rating of movies—but she largely followed the judgment of the German historian Winckelmann.)

Similarly, by the time Emerson arrived travelers had developed prejudices about the Italians themselves. These grew more negative as visitors became more numerous but less purposeful. The middle classes were arriving, if not yet in "shoals," then in regular numbers, and they brought their Protestant, bourgeois prejudices with them. The Anglophones tended to perceive the natives as childlike, their religion as superstitious, and their society as of little worth. Italians, in truth, were generally poorer than their visitors, and they did not generally entertain foreigners lavishly, if at all. The story went around that the local people after a party would send their servants to guests, demanding payment—and Emerson seems to have run into a form of this custom. Apparently it was the servants' initiative to seek these fees, but, as Baker has shown, equally some families were understood to pay no wages and let their help fend for themselves.

Partly as a result, but fundamentally because it is a law of nature that nationals in strange lands clot together, the English, French, German, and American visitors developed their own favored gathering places in the major cities. They lodged in the same hotels, shared their *vetture*, and accompanied each other in visiting the sights. Byron noticed with horror how his countrymen "infected" Florence in *1818*, making it a "Lazaretto"—a place of quarantine to be avoided—but of course it was to an Englishman that he wrote; and it was to Shelley, another English milord and poet, that he loaned his rented villa in the Euganean Hills.*

Emerson too fell in with other Americans, but he kept an open mind. Far from feeling intolerant toward Catholicism—then an invasive religion, unwelcome in Puritan New England—he was immediately enthralled by its monuments and favorably impressed by its priests. He went, like the best travelers before him, if not precisely naked into this new experience, at least deliberately vulnerable, almost *incognito*, not concealing but not advertising his ministerial calling. He deliberately traveled without the conventional guidebooks, such as Starke or Forsyth. He also left home his Virgil and Plutarch—classical authors who had stepped on the very ground he now crossed—and occasionally he felt he wanted them. The works he did consult and copy into his journals were geographies packed with useful statistics, neutral in tone. The reason was that he had come to walk on his own feet and see with his own eyes; this was not the time for more study, but for life.

*George Gordon, Lord Byron, *Byron's Letters and Journals*, ed. Leslie A. Marchand, *11* vols. (London: John Murray, *1973–81*), *6:65*.

MALTA

AFTER thirty-eight days at sea, which drew to a close as they passed Gibraltar and coasted near enough Africa and Spain to see fishermen's fires on both sides, the *Jasper* anchored in St. Paul's Bay in Malta. An island colony of England, it was a normal first port of call for trading vessels bound for Italy, but if Emerson had planned it, he could not have chosen a landfall more exotic and feudal. And, as he remarked, "to enter Europe at the little end" was an advantage, "so we shall admire by just degrees from the Maltese architecture up to St. Peter's."

They were shut up in quarantine for two weeks, but even this tedious period had its oddities, and Emerson described

> . . . the Parlatorio, where those in quarantine converse with those out across barriers. It looked to me like the wildest masquerade. There jabbered Turks, Moors, Sicilians, Germans, Greeks, English, Maltese, with friars & guards & maimed & beggars. And such grotesque faces! It resembled more some brave antique picture than a congregation of flesh & blood.

Malta's three inhabited islands lie strategically in the Mediterranean some sixty miles south of Sicily, and the archipelago has been a crossing point for trade and war since prehistoric Phoenician times. Receiving only small amounts of rainfall largely in winter, its soil is a thin carpet over massive limestone and sandstone escarpments, but this weathers when quarried to a fine butter-yellow that darkens with age to gold. From this stone—so soft that it not only yields to the chisel but accepts oils for frescoes, as the painter Mattia Preti discovered—builders since the sixteenth century have constructed the battlements and carved the massive buildings. These and their ornaments were for centuries the pride of the West, for since the Crusades Malta had been a staging place for European campaigns against the Ottoman Empire.

Valletta rises from the peak of a mountain above a series of extraordinary harbors, deeply indented, bordered by almost vertical cliffs, and topped by great batteries and garrisons that train their eyes seaward. Since Jean de la Valette, after whom the city was named, had defeated the Turks in a bloody siege in 1565, knights from every Catholic country had made it a point of honor to gain a toehold in this freebooting garrison city. They erected grandly baroque "auberges" for themselves, princely barracks not unlike medieval colleges, rectangular in shape with central courtyards, dining halls decorated with carved escutcheons and trophies, massive walls pierced by great doors, and stone staircases wide enough for regiments to march through.

The Knights of Malta, originally celibate members of the Order of St. John, had ruled the country since the king of Spain had given it to them in 1530. The native Maltese were and are a particularly devout populace, but over the centuries the knights grew lazy, corrupt, and licentious, and they lost control of the civil government. Only a generation before Emerson arrived, Malta had fallen to Napoleon and then quickly passed into English hands. The rule of the Order of the Knights of Malta—with its annual tribute of a falcon given in symbolic fealty to the Spanish king—was no more. By the time Emerson arrived, Malta was an English possession. But for centuries the Grand Masters of the Order had established their magnificence by building churches and cathedrals as well as public works, and great architects and artists like Preti and Caravaggio had been among their employees.

To Emerson it was all a wonder, and as soon as he was released from his watery prison he plunged into this new culture. At once he reported that though he knew it was "very green and juvenile," he had perambulated from one end to the other of "this little town of stone," this "box of curiosities," unable to "keep my eyes from rolling . . . in their sockets nor my tongue from uttering my pleasure & surprize."

He made straight for the most imposing of all the Maltese monuments, the great Co-Cathedral of St. John, begun by la Valette and adorned through the centuries by his successors. It was Emerson's first exposure to Catholic religious architecture on its natal ground, and his response was immediate and happy. It was "a noble house to worship God in; the walls are eloquent with texts & the floor covered with epitaphs. . . ." He noticed especially how open and frequented (still a fact in Malta) the many churches were:

> I yielded me joyfully to the religious impression of holy texts & fine paintings & this soothfast faith though of women & children. How beautiful to have the

church always open, so that every tired wayfaring man may come in & be soothed by all that art can suggest of a better world when he is weary with this.

Not only was this son of the Covenanters not offended by rich ecclesiastical embellishment, he longed for it: "I hope they will carve & paint & inscribe the walls of our churches in New England." And finally, "How could anybody who had been in a catholic church, devise such a deformity as a pew?"

He visited this and other churches repeatedly, and it was here that he first heard the sound of chanting friars: "The music of the organ & chaunting friars very impressive, especially when we left the kneeling congregation in the nave, & heard it at a distance, as we examined the pictures in a side oratory." That experience perhaps became part of his poem "The Problem," which welled up and was set down virtually unchanged some six years later, and begins with a memory of those monastic aisles, suffused in song:

I like a church; I like a cowl;
I love a prophet of the soul;
And on my heart monastic aisles
Fall like sweet strains, or pensive smiles . . .

He attended mass, and thought the bishop "a venerable old man." But though he found much to admire, he drew the line at one of the oldest of the Reformation's sticking points, "the description over the gate, '*Indulgentia, plenaria, quotidiana, perpetua, pro vivis et defunctis*' ["Indulgence, full, daily, perpetual, for the living and the dead"]. This is almost too frank, may it please your holiness." (In fact, the inscription may still be read over the porch of St. Francis of Assisi on Republic Street, the main thoroughfare of Valletta.)

He reacted to the central presence in Malta of the "living rock"—what he called "this cold, clean, sightly stone." Visiting a sculptor, he imagined that "if I had a great house in America, I would send to the Signor [Dimeck] for a pair of vases which I saw"—four feet high, two feet around, richly carved. He did not wait to be rich, happily; his account book shows that he ordered the vases.

English-speaking society in Malta was readily open to meeting and being entertained by its visitors. The temperature was in the mid-fifties, though it was early February, and in a few days he managed not only repeated visits to the cathedral and churches, but also to the chapel of the English missionary Mr. Temple (probably located cozily next to the cathedral at 33 Tesorio Street); to the Armory, a hall perhaps two hundred feet long, mounted with "the arms of the old knights of every form & size"—great hollow men of steel, hung up in all their dry menace; and to the great National Library. He even made a social call upon the wife of the local doctor, John Davy, brother of the well-known Sir Humphry Davy.

He missed one encounter, however, that would have been interesting, for John Henry Newman—the English divine who was moving away from orthodoxy just as Emerson had done, but in the opposite direction, toward conversion to Catholicism—was in Malta in the same time, as reported in *The Malta Government Gazette* (13 Feb. *1833*). Emerson was shut up in quarantine, however, until after the charismatic Anglican had left for Sicily. Later their paths were to cross again, for both were in St. Peter's for Easter service, but these two men, whose careers were mirror images of each other, were destined not to meet.

Before Emerson himself left for Sicily, he attended a fancy dress ball given by the English governor to which he'd been invited through the courtesy of the American consul. It may have been Emerson's first such experience, for he had lived in poverty as a boy, and very quietly as a grown man married to a dying wife, himself fighting sickness, and soon deep grief at her loss. He enjoyed the ball—"a very gay and novel scene,"—but it was not up to the place (the palace itself, a great baroque building that was formerly the Auberge de Provence), or to his "expectation." Some pleasures should be tasted young.

He reflected on a young girl he'd noticed, one of "a few beautiful faces in the dancing crowd, & a beautiful face is always worth going far to see." He was not unsusceptible, but he needed to see "the *moral*" in beauty, and the fleeting vision he took away was of "a long descended maiden . . . of an immaculate innocence, a sort of wild virtue . . . wild & fragrant as the violets." Finding that in those halls, he was "surprised & gratified with the strong contrast—meeting the Divinity amidst flowers & trifles."

Perhaps he was spending his time better, after all, than in disputations with the Reverend Newman.

At any rate, Malta was waking him up. Mount Etna could be seen on fair days raising its white cone over the Tyrrhenian Sea. Emerson was drawn northward. Six days after his release from quarantine, he was again aboard ship, bound for Syracuse on the east coast of Sicily—the landing place for travelers since its days as a chief city in Magna Graecia; the home of Archimedes; the place where the buried river Arethusa rose up from the sea in legendary fashion, a nymph escaping from her pursuer's hounds, a subterranean current linking Greece with her valued colony.

~ "Malta Illustrata." "*The library of the Knights contains 40000 volumes, and a venerable ptolemaic bookstall it is. I sat down & read in Abela's old folios—'Melita Illustrata.'*"

teu'io desiderargli, quant'il vederla riceuuta sotto l'ali augu...
stime di quell'AQVILA, che solleuandosi ben spesso fino alla...
ra del Sole, e della gloria più sublime à prouedersi di luce, e...
fulmini, non lascia dubitarmi, che non sia per contribui...
influssi benigni di protettione, e non dargli ancora co'suoi...
dori quel lustro, che non hà potuto sortire dalla mia tropp'o...
ra penna. Oltre che hauendo i gloriosi Antecessori della sua...
perial Famiglia de LASCARIS tenuto già il possesso dell'Im...
rio Orientale, e disteso lo scettro anche à quest'Isola mia Pat...
è ben giusto, ch'ora si continui, e si raddoppij all'Em. V. ne...
scritti. Gradiscagli però benignamente V.Em. (ch'io ne la sup...
co.) E pregando il Sig. Iddio di conseruare la sua Eminen...
Persona, e di felicitarla sempre maggiormente, le faccio pro...
dissimo inchino.

Nella Città Valletta li 10. di Luglio 1647.

Di V. Eminenza

Humiliss, e diuotiss, religioso, e seruitore, vassallo fed...

Fr. Gio: Francesc...

DELLA DESCRITTIONE DI MALTA,
DEL COMMENDATOR ABELA
Libro Primo.

DEL SITO DELL'ISOLA,
e di tutto il suo Littorale.

NOTITIA PRIMA.

L'Isola di Malta famosa, e celebre non meno per la residenza della Sacra, & Eminentiss. Religione Gierosolimitana (di cui habbiamo l'honore di portarne l'habito,) che per la natural fortezza del Sito, e per la commodità, e sicurezza de'porti; In vece d'Ercole, e di Giunone hoggi sacrata al glorioso Apostolo S. Paolo, protetta dal nostro Tutelare Precursor di Christo; fù Colonia de Fenici potenti nel mare; di presente habitatione de'più Celebri, & Illustri Eroi Christiani, Fenici di gloria, e di valore, fregiati della bianca croce. E stata commemorata da molti Scrittori Greci, e Latini; ma hoggidì predicata per Antemurale, e Propugnacolo del Christianesimo; le sue estrinseche parti formano la figura d'vn pesce. Ella è situata in alto mare, lontana più ch'alcun'altra da terra ferma nell'Vmbilico del Mediterraneo, al lato meridionale di Sicilia, trà Pachino hoggi Capo Passaro, e Camarana anticamente Camerina colonia di Siracusa; dalla parte di tramontana risguarda la Sicilia al dirimpetto del Pozzallo; da mezzo giorno l'Africa verso Tripoli; da leuante la Candia, e da ponente il Gozo; dal

A   Settentrione

~ St. John's Cathedral, Valletta, Malta. *"I went to St. John's Church & a noble house it is to worship God in; full of marble & mosaic & pictures & gilding. . . . "*

~ St. John's Cathedral, marble intarsia on floor.

D   O   M

F FRANCISCUS GIACHE DE CALAN
BAIUL ET TEMPLI DE M VILION COMMEND
EQUES MAIORU VIRUM
DE SIC IN E VIRTUTI O STRENUUS AEMULATUR
FREMISSIS SIBI MUNERIBUS
ATQUE OP VI SIUS VICTORIUS E ALIIS
LITTORALI O CONTIGIO
AC OFELIS FL CONTARU GENERALIS INSPECTOR
CAMERA ORNACEDIALI ETIAM QUAESTURA
EGREGIE FUNCTUS
SEMET VIRUM EXIBUI PRAESTANTISSIMUM
OI
MILI ALAMI ATE AI QUTUS
DUABUS MISSI C MELI PUIU ACELLO

~ St. John's Bastion, Malta.

"A.D. 1523 [1530] *ceded by Charles V to the Knights of Rhodes*
under the Grand Master L'Isle Adam
1565 *repelled the Turks*
1798 *submitted to France*
1800 *capitulated to England*"

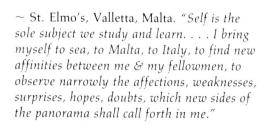

~ St. Elmo's, Valletta, Malta. *"Self is the sole subject we study and learn. . . . I bring myself to sea, to Malta, to Italy, to find new affinities between me & my fellowmen, to observe narrowly the affections, weaknesses, surprises, hopes, doubts, which new sides of the panorama shall call forth in me."*

SICILY

THE trip in the little ship from Malta to Sicily amused and opened the eyes of this New Englander. The sailors tended the ship as needed without instructions, drank their wine when they wished, and made jokes at the captain's expense. The cabin boy had ridiculously trivial duties and got knocked on the head by everyone when he made a mistake, while the captain not only accepted familiarity, but actually took the helmsman's place "affectionately" while the latter had supper. And everyone amused himself "mightily" by observing the passengers. Nevertheless, he noticed, "the little vessel sailed fast" and when they reached customs at Syracuse, "the Captain & mate helped us all they could, & our money opened all the gates at last."

In short, Emerson—still traveling with the four Americans from the *Jasper*—was getting a crash course on this crossing in Italian character and mores: a preference for improvisation, a certain sabotage of rigid class boundaries, and along with this seeming anarchy, an elastic good nature. Even what they ate drew his attention: *purpo*, a lobsterlike fish, bread, green onions, and red wine.

IT was spring when he stepped ashore to Sicily's gentle welcome. Finding himself in ancient Syracuse induced a delight close to giddiness, and he remarked that like the Berber in Rome, "the greatest wonder of all [is] to find myself here." He took lodgings in the Strada Amalfitana, a short street leading down to the harbor in the old peninsular town known as Ortygia—Greek for quail, both a common local bird and similar to the shape of the peninsula itself—and in late February he wrote his brother:

~ Cloister, San Giovanni degli Eremiti, Palermo.

27

[I] date a letter to you from this oldest of towns. Here have I been dwelling . . . with Mt. Etna visible from one window, the pillars of the temple of . . . Jove from another, & the tomb of Archimedes & the Ear of Dionysius [a cavern used as a prison by an ancient tyrant] from the house top. I have drunk the waters of the Fountain Arethusa; I have plucked the Papyrus on the banks of the Anapus; I have visited the same Catacombs which Cicero admired. . . . I have heard mass said in the ancient temple of Minerva now converted into a cathedral. For my breakfast they give me most fragrant Hyblaean honey; & quails (in Ortygia) for dinner.

From Mount Etna to the honey of Hybla, all these had once been merely words they had studied in school. What overwhelmed Emerson was the sense of intimacy with the classical past that he felt in this city—now decayed and shrunk almost to its size at its founding 2,500 years before, and far smaller than the several hundred thousand it had grown to in its days of glory. Archimedes had made his calculations here; Aeschylus had produced a play in a theater that still emanated an ideal Greek serenity. Even Plato, who had taught that philosophers should be kings, had lived here, imprisoned by the same Dionysius when he had gotten himself mixed up in real Greco-Syracusan politics.

On his street was a café (perhaps the same one that exists there now) whose frescoes showed Archimedes using a windlass to pull a galley. A short distance to the left, by the water, he came on the famous fountain of Arethusa—now, alas, turned into a general washing tub where "fifty or sixty women were polluting it with all the filthy clothes of the city." The same pollution had been noticed by Goethe and Brydone in the eighteenth century.

The American consul, an Italian named Signor Ricciardi, courteously called on Emerson's party the day after they arrived and took them around the sights: to the supposed Tomb of Archimedes, to the Greek and Roman theaters, to all the remnants of tyrants who had lived eons before—now turned, like the fountain, to ordinary uses. In the great damp cavern known as "Dionysius's Ear" because of its whispering-chamber acoustics, a group of twinemakers now worked. In open quarries, great pits known as *latomie* stretched for acres. Once prisons quarried by Greek prisoners for stone to build the city, now they grew sunken groves of oranges and lemons, so that visitors looked not out but down at that Shelleyan "emerald sky of leaves" and starry fruit.

The shock through it all was the denseness of history, of events crowded so thickly into this small space that their remains jostled each other like a crowd of unceremonious people jammed together. The Duomo was a stunning example. Built 2,500 years earlier by the Greek colonists as the Temple of Athena, it still stands as it was erected six centuries before Christ, twelve massive Doric columns rising powerful and strong on each side of the architrave of pitted, fossil-filled limestone. In long succession, one ruler succeeded another: Greeks, Romans, Vandals, Visigoths, and Arabs, they came in waves, held sway for centuries, and then gave way. But when at last the Normans took Sicily from the Arabs in the eleventh century, they bricked in the space between the temple's columns—which are still entirely visible—and roofed it all over with their characteristic battlement in the right-angled sawtooth pattern called machicolated that enables defending archers to shoot or pour combustibles downward while sheltering behind the vertical teeth. And then, yet more centuries later, the Spanish conquered and had their turn: this ancient building whose foundations on the street side speak so unmistakably to the passerby of a nearly prehistoric origin now had a seventeenth-century Spanish Flamboyant façade, all heavy carving and formal show, made to match the style of the other grand buildings on the piazza. Nothing can prepare an American to turn such a corner and move in one right angle through two thousand years; one must see it for oneself.

Just beyond the Duomo begins the ancient ghetto, its streets so narrow that in places one may stand in the middle and touch both walls at once. In this mazy city time has not so much stood still as intensified, till wandering through it is like sipping the local coffee: only a tablespoon or two in the bottom of a tiny cup, but intense, aromatic, and dark as the bottom of a well.

Emerson remarked on the ironies of time, wondering if it was "grand or mournful that I should hear mass in this Temple of Minerva this morn. . . . Is it not good witness to the ineradicableness of the religious principle? In these regions," he added, "every where they confound pagan & Christian Antiquity & half preserve both."

He visited a monastery high above the city that looks down at the great harbor and was enchanted by the air, the view, and the quiet: "I told the Padre that I would stay there always if he would give me a chamber. He said, 'I should have his', which he opened—a little neat room, with a few books." Then Emerson added, "My friend's whipcords hung by the bed side." Little was lost on him, and nothing overstated.

Later that day they were visited by another monk, bearded and barefoot, bearing a dish of olives and lemons, who invited them to join him in walking to yet another monastery and its *latomie*, an excursion they gladly took. He was a capuchin from the Church of San Giovanni, whose sanctuary had been built and rebuilt over a temple fully as ancient as that in the center of the city, for the Church of St. John, ruined by earthquakes repeatedly, has in its lowest crypt not only pagan catacombs, but a temple dedicated to Demeter.

Everywhere Emerson was conscious that he was walking in the world of legend, and bits of Cicero and Plutarch came back to him as he walked. Taking a boat up the River Anapus, he walked almost to the spot where " 'gloomy Dis' " had stamped his foot and ravished Proserpine down to the underworld. "No wonder Proserpine gathered flowers," Emerson remarked, "they grow everywhere of prettiest forms & liveliest colors now in February, & I stopped ever & anon to pick them."

Almost as famous among moderns for its decay as for its history, paradoxically Syracuse was for Emerson a place where spring reigned. The warmth, the sunlight, the welcome of the people, the dishes of olives and lemons, the growing fruit itself, the papyrus he also gathered, the fragrant Hyblaean honey he had with his break- fast—all creep half-consciously into his tale till they spill out, as in the catalogue of sensuous growth he found in the garden of a friendly marchese:

> The rich soil is now filled with flowers in wildest profusion of scent & color. The bergamot, lemon, the orange, the citron, we plucked & ate; & lavender & rosemary & roses & hyacinths & jasmine & thyme, which were running wild all over the grounds we filled our hands & hats with.

"Still, melancholy, old metropolis! under the moon, last eve, how wan & grey it looked." But his hands were not enough to hold the riches this sense-starved New Englander took up even into his hat. No wonder Proserpine gathered flowers.

THE cities of Sicily hug the shore of this triangular island, and Emerson's itinerary was to take him along two sides of it. Catania lay a long day's journey north of Syracuse and almost under the volcano, of which he was always conscious. "Fine air, clear sun, Mt. Aetna right before us," he reported of the beginning, and again, later, "flowers abounding, the road smooth and Aetna glorious to behold with his cap of smoke, & the Mountainettes like warts all over his huge sides." The road they followed was in part the seashore itself, a "beach like that of Lynn, paved with pretty shells."

A thirteen-hour day, some of it on foot, fording streams, and mud that felled even the mules did not deter him: "the sun set, the moon rose, and still we did not reach the town," but

> . . . the bay of Naples cannot be so beautiful as the spacious bay [of Catania], round the shore of which we straggled & stumbled with tinkling mules, & sighing & shouting drivers. Tzar, Tzar, gia, hm, and many an odd, nondescript, despairing sound they utter to that deliberate animal.

The rhythm of travel had established itself, and with it, physical strength and the beginnings of inner harmony. The world—its fine air, its flowery scents, the sounds made by the muleteers—was more and more alive around him and in his language.

Catania was a thriving city of 70,000 spread out on the plain below Etna. White above with snow and smoke eternally pouring from its throat, girdled about the shoulders by forests and at its lap by meadows and citrus groves, the mountain speaks at once of beauty and menace. Black basaltic stones litter its fields, close its roads, and spill down into the sea, leaving columns of lava to be eaten forever by the lapping waves. Emerson had been observing it since arriving in Valletta, and he took it that it had a message for him:

> Town of lava and earthquakes. The mountain is at once a monument & a warning. Houses are built, streets paved with lava; it is polished in the altars of the churches. Huge black rocks of it line the shore, & the white surf breaks over them.

The monument was to death; the warning was—to choose life.

It was in recognition of this choice that on the day after he arrived there Emerson wrote out in his journal—rough and unfinished, but genuine—the first poem he had composed in months, even years:

> We are what we are made & every following day
> Is the Creator of our human mould
> Not less than was the first. God
> Gilds a few points in every several life
> And as each flower
> And every varied leaf is sketched each with a new design
> A spot of purple & a streak of brown
> So each man's life its own beauty shall have
> And a few peculiar delights . . .
> . . . & reconcile him to the common days
> Not many men I suppose see any pleasure in
> The fogs of close low pine woods in a river
> town Yet unto me not star's magnificence
> nor the red rainbow of a summer's day nor Rome
> nor Paris nor splendid festal parlours nor
> the wit of man nor angels' music hath such a
> soul a resurrection of the happy past
> As comes to me when I see the morning in
> such low moist roadside where blue violets peep
> as magic remembrances out of the black loam

It is a poem of reconciliation, of acceptance of the self for what it is in God's care, moved by a sense of life and of the burgeoning spring. When he revised it a few weeks later in Naples, he added the name that underlay the sadness and the references to the "resurrection of the happy past"—that of Ellen, his young wife, dead at age nineteen. In Syracuse he had gathered too many flowers for his hands to hold; now in Catania they poured out of his words—blue violets (like the wild innocence of Ellen and the beauty in Valletta), "A spot of purple & a streak of brown," and "The fogs of close low pine woods in a river/town."

IN Catania at St. Agatha's and later in the Benedictine monastery, Emerson for the first time visited an entirely Italian cathedral. It surpassed anything he had encountered, and he was awed and exhilarated by the scale: "We feel so little & so elated upon the floor." He sounded a theme he was to repeat: "Have the men of America never entered these European churches that they build such mean edifices at home? . . . O the marbles! & oh the pictures & oh the noble proportions of the pile!"

Why could not America build like this? At home the Puritan vision had for centuries insisted upon a religious architecture in which the white light of day lit up the rectangular boxes of pews, and the church was formed on an open plan with a gallery running on three sides of a squarish hall. For color there might be a little upholstery—or there might not. Flowers were permitted, but as late as his father's day, parishes had rejected instrumental music, even to accompany the hymns. (William Emerson had tried to use the cello during services in his country church but was defeated by his parishioners.) In that space all could be seen at once; there was to be no mystery save in the worshipper's heart or the language of the text. There might be beauty, harmony, and a sense of peace in such a building, but Emerson now saw its limitations.

Here the space was divided by long parallel aisles with innumerable chapels, large and small, dark and light, ranged along the sides and tucked away behind the altar, each with its own character, altar, artwork, candles, and kneeling devout—this structure spoke of the many in one, of particular and private impulses all guided and governed by a shared dedication to the central purpose. In such a church, filled with song, fragrant with incense, lit with jewellike light filtered through richly colored lead-glass windows, and immensely decorated by carving, by intarsia work using inlaid stone of many colors, and by flamboyant plate and statuary arranged so that the light and shadows glinted on them and their drama—this use of space suggested not only theater, but multitudinousness, a denseness of imagery and of the creative spirit that would be hard to penetrate, a mystery defying simplification.

Emerson was never attracted to Catholicism per se, but the language of art spoke piercingly to him, and he responded almost with envy and a prediction that America would herself build such temples before the century was over.

He did not, however, lose his critical intelligence. The edifice was mighty, but he commented:

> Indeed, my holy Fathers, your vows of poverty & humility have cost you little. . . . this morn I called upon his reverence in his cell, & the kings of France & England, I think, do not live in a better house. . . . About 50 monks are laid up in clover & magnificence here.

He followed this with an understated criticism that simply recorded the facts: "I saw hundreds of women & children in the yard each receiving her loaf & passing on into a court, that none should come twice to the basket."

BY the end of his stay in this city, Emerson had reached a personal plateau. He had been away for over two months. The sea journey and its rigors were behind him, and in the last three weeks he had moved through two countries, among foreigners, mixing with governors, consuls, and men and women of a stripe he did not know at home. His strength was unflagging, his health excellent. He made no complaints about either the food or his lodging. Clearly, he was adapting well and developing new accomplishments. If his Italian was weak—especially when he matched his Tuscan dialect against the Sicilian—he could at least make himself understood. Despite—or perhaps because of—the constant work of travel, he found himself happier and healthier than he had been in a long time.

He was ready to move out on his own, and this he did in the beginning of March, parting company from the Holbrook family and Samuel Kettell and engaging a carriage to take him as far as Messina. He spent the night at a little dark inn on the beach, where the roar of the sea lulled him to sleep, and awoke to find Taormina high overhead, so high and steep it seemed inaccessible, "and if men could get there, not safe to live on the edge of a rock." Get to that exquisite town he did, with its magnificent Greek theater and vision of Etna. In March he wrote his brother's fiancée:

> I am very easy to please. I hardly pass a monastery but I ask them on what terms they will receive me for life, and in Sicily when I saw them taking cicinelli, I had half a mind to be a fisherman and draw my net at Taormina the rest of my days.

He asked only for good weather, good views, a "little coffee," and "calm civil people" to be content. The "calm civil people" included his memory of his companions in his rented coach: a priest, his two nephews, and a third man, all kind and generous with provisions and attentions. Their "intercourse with me was all a comedy. . . . When I could not understand they would raise their voices, and then all say the same thing." The priest thought of trying Latin instead, but they found that did not work, given his Sicilian accent. When the entire household had gathered around to help, the coachman told them Emerson was also a priest in his own country.

> This was wonders more. Then at every sentence which I forged and uttered was profound silence followed by acclamations "che bravo Signore!" so modulated as only Italians can.

From Messina, Emerson planned to sail to Palermo, and from there embark for Naples. It was a pleasant prospect. He made the short sea voyage in less than a day. The route took him between Scylla and Charybdis, and then gave a sight of the summit of Stromboli, near the Lipari islands, its crater smoking and glowing at night with a faint, fiery light. He met a trio of Englishmen on board and found them, contrary to report, "courteous," although the empire-building English had then a reputation for bad manners.

Palermo—"a fine sight from the sea" with its "bold mountainous coast"—was, with *168,000* inhabitants, the largest city Emerson had yet entered. In fact, it was almost the largest city he had visited anywhere, for Boston's population then was around *61,000*, and in America only New York had reached the *200,000* mark. The size did not dismay him, however, for he was learning how to travel and arrange to see what he wished without fuss. Within the space of three days he visited the major attractions—in addition to numerous fine churches, the cathedral, the Viceroy's (now the Governor's) Palace with its Norman chapel, the "noble" public gardens, and the fine marina or local harbor. He regretted a trip to the hospital for tuberculosis, to which his guide led him unawares, for as he remarked, "I could not help them & have seen enough of their sad malady without coming to Sicily."

One of the excursions he liked best was a visit to the Capuchin "convent" (it was customary to use that term as we would employ "monastery"), for they were the "most esteemed of the Catholic clergy." "Their profession is beggary," he reported, "but they distribute large alms to the poor." His trip included exploring the bizarre catacombs that lie beneath this monastery on the outskirts of the city. He had a soft spot for catacombs and seldom missed a chance to enter them, but this one was and is unique, for it contains centuries' worth of mummified monks hung up in niches carved from the rock, their brown robes bearing the dust of ages still draped about skeletal shoulders:

> Hundreds & hundreds of these grinning mortalities were ranged along the walls, here an abbot, there a General of the Convent. Every one had his label with his name, when in the body, hanging at his breast. One was near *300* years old. On some the beard remained, on some the hair. I asked the monk how many there were? He said, since *300* years half a million; and he himself would stand there with his brothers in his turn.

The same "grinning mortalities" still hang there, but they have been joined by a host of well-dressed Palermitans in full visiting costume, for in the mid-nineteenth century it evidently became fashionable to assemble with the poor friars in this great antechamber to immortality. There is a special room for the beruffled skeletal infants of this class; signs point the visitor to the interesting spectacle.

In general there was little in Palermo to fix Emerson's imagination. With an extra day's wait for the ship he was at last to take to the mainland, he climbed to Monreale, some five miles distant, and visited the glorious cathedral there, but though he thought the landscape beautiful, he was out of superlatives to spend on churches for a while. His mind was probably fixed on the next leg of his journey—which was to be for the first time by steam, not sail, and would put him at the very center of the classical Italian world, Naples.

~ Lava landscape, road near Mount Etna, Sicily.

~ Mount Etna, Sicily. *"Fine air, clear sun, Mount Aetna right before us, green fields—laborers ploughing in them, many flowers, all the houses of stone."*

~ San Giovanni, Syracuse, Sicily. *"Then went to the Church—very old, small, & poor; but by stone stairs descended into one far older, which they say is St John's Church, & coeval with the planting of Christianity in Sicily."*

~ Detail of San Giovanni. *"The bold carving of the granite all around made me think it of Greek age & afterwards converted to this use."*

~ Temple of Minerva, now the Duomo, Syracuse, Sicily. *"Shall I count it like the Berber at Rome the greatest wonder of all to find myself here? I have this day . . . been into the old temple of Minerva praised for its beauty by Cicero & now preserved & concealed by having its pillars half buried in the walls of the Cathedral."*

~ Landscape, Calascibetta, Sicily. *"...& my Sicilian companions would break out 'O che bella veduta!'"*

~ Riviera dei Ciclopi, Sicily. *"Catania. Town of lava of earthquakes. . . . Huge black rocks of it line the shore, and the white surf breaks over them."*

NAPLES

EMERSON had looked forward especially to Naples, for of all the Italian cities, its reputation was the most glamorous. From classical to modern times, it had been a center of history, a plum to be won by intrigue and war. The unearthing of Pompeii in the mid-eighteenth century made it a magnet for all the traveling cognoscenti of the Western world. Winckelmann had studied its ruins; Goethe had triumphed there. At the turn of the century Lord Nelson had sailed victorious into its harbor and been the guest of the aging Sir William Hamilton and his beautiful young mistress Emma in their grand villa overlooking the bay—a visit that was the prelude to a famous romance. It was considered the most beautiful of all cities, with the finest climate and greatest harbor. *"Vedi Napoli et poi muori"* was the common phrase, which Emerson quoted while boning up before arriving. But despite all this, it was to be the low point of Emerson's voyage. As he remarked toward the end of his stay there in the tone of a sadder but wiser man: "It takes one 'Grand tour' to learn how to travel."

In its favor was its setting: an enormous bay, arching fifty miles from Baia on the west to Sorrento on the east, marked far out to sea by the volcanic islands of Capri and Ischia, and ringed by the villas and temples of patrician rulers since the days when it was founded by the Greeks as the New City or Ne-polis—hence, Napoli. Palm trees edged the shore; flowers flourished most of the year in the rich volcanic soil. Even today, only Genoa has more trade in its harbor. Vesuvius rises above it almost 9,000 feet high to the east, impressive even when silent, but usually alive and smoking. When the writers Emerson knew best had traveled there in the seventeenth

~ Casa di Menandro, Pompeii. *"Long ago when I dreamed at home of these things, I thought I should come suddenly in the midst of an open country upon broken columns & fallen friezes. . . ."*

49

and eighteenth centuries, the waters of the bay were clear and exquisitely blue, full of pleasure craft, trading vessels, and swimmers, the shore thronged by idlers—the famous *lazzaroni*—enjoying its beauty.

It had been a resort since classical times. Pliny the historian had lived there; so had Virgil, who, though a native of Mantua, chose to have his ashes preserved on the hill of Posilipo on the western side of the bay. Augustus, Tiberius, and Nero all had had summer palaces there, for the climate was milder than Rome's and the air healthier.

In modern days too Naples was noted for gaiety, music, and love of pleasure, the home of *bel canto*. Still a kingdom governed by Ferdinand II of the Two Sicilies when Emerson arrived, peasants and nobility alike shared a devotion to spectacle. They especially celebrated the famous feast of Piedigrotta, held at a church near a Roman tunnel cut through the mountain, close to the magnificent public gardens facing the bay. On one such *festa, 350,000* people dressed in rich finery turned out to see the king in his gold-plated coach lead a cortège of forty more, with *15,000* Austrian soldiers bringing up the rear. Now the air is thick with smog from nearby refineries, and the streets and gardens are shabby with dirty façades and broken pavement. But in the early nineteenth century, the rich flocked to the grand apartments overlooking the parade route near the bay and paid almost a year's rent for a few nights, merely to entertain their friends and watch the glittering show from windows and balconies.*

Emerson did not arrive in time for this *festa*, but he did attend the opera in the San Carlo theater, which had been rebuilt after a fire in *1816*. It is still one of the world's largest theaters, but it has far more charm and intimacy than modern halls, for it is built not deep, but high and round, with six tiers of boxes decorated in red plush, cream, and gilt.

Naples was famous for its street life, its sounds and songs adding to its reputation for vitality and charm. Goethe catalogued at least ten eccentric trades he watched being carried on in the open. He capped his observations—which he interpreted as evidence of the thrifty and inventive Neapolitan spirit—by describing a circle of street urchins squatted on the road, their palms to the stones: an artisan had just done forging a wheel, and they had gathered to warm themselves.

But there was another side to this long history of natural favor. The city's very splendor had drawn the populace to it like a magnet, and it was vastly overcrowded even in the *1830*s, filled with destitute people who had become homeless beggars. Emerson could not harden himself to their devastating poverty. "Goethe says 'he shall never again be wholly unhappy, for he has seen Naples.' " But that had been

*Desmond Seward, *Naples: A Travellers' Companion* (New York: Atheneum, *1986*), *207–208*.

50

more than forty years earlier, and Emerson could not "go five yards in any direction without seeing saddest objects & hearing the most piteous wailings. . . . Whilst you eat your dinner at a Trattoria, a beggar stands at the window, watching every mouthful."

In addition, the climate, though not malarial, was known for its rainy springs; in some seasons, according to Brydone, it rained every day for six or seven weeks.* Emerson was caught in this sirocco, and in mid-March he encountered the coldest, wettest weather of his trip. He was there for two weeks, and it rained chilly gusts almost every day.

Moreover, the city was full of travelers, and though he changed hotels seeking a better one, he, the uncomplaining, described his inn as "my black lodgings," and a night's entertainment as staying in it and reading Goethe. Yet it was an improvement over his previous hotel near the waterfront and Santa Lucia, where opposite his window, on the "4th story, a family lived with poultry cackling around them all day, 40 feet from the ground." But even in new accommodations in the Croce di Malta, "I observe a turkey in the chamber across the street stepping about the 2nd story. A goat comes up stairs every day to be milked."

Equally important was the fact that he was no longer stopping in a provincial city where a simple visit to the American consul or his banker made him part of the social scene. Even wealthy English travelers like Brydone had found little in common with Neapolitans. Their solution, like Emerson's, was to concentrate on the natural and antique objects of interest.

Emerson was at first intimidated by the high style of this city six times the size of Boston. He had to remind himself not to be dazzled by his hotel, or jostled from his course by being stared at "by dozens of idlers in the street" and judged on the state of his shoes and hat. He felt defensive and tried to pep himself up:

> It is so easy . . . to be overawed by names that on entering this bay it is hard to keep one's judgment upright. . . . Here's for the plain old Adam, the simple genuine Self against the whole world. Need is, that you assert yourself or you will find yourself overborne. . . .

But worse lay ahead. The classical sites made famous by Virgil and other writers were strung out along the eastern side of the bay. There lay the smoking cave of the sybil of Cuma; there the dark tarn of Lake Avernus, there the Solfatura—all the fearsome sites of the Phlegraean Fields, products of subterranean volcanic action, which the Romans had associated with death and the underworld. There was a

*Patrick Brydone, *A Tour Through Sicily and Malta in a Series of Letters to William Beckford, Esq.* (London: Cadell & Davies, 1806), 4.

~ Church of San Martino, Naples. *"Have the men of America never entered these European churches that they build such mean edifices at home? . . . But O the marbles! & oh the pictures & oh the noble proportions of the pile!"*

Overleaf:

~ *Socrates*, National Museum, Naples *(left).*

~ *Homer*, National Museum, Naples *(right).*

dignity to their image. As Emerson remarked truly, "We always look at volcanoes with great respect." But he was to find that long centuries of decay and abuse had turned these locations into heaps of rubble, scabbed over by the ephemeral dwellings of the poor, a treeless, broken, and melancholy waste.

Emerson went out to Pozzuoli and the Grotto del Cane, part of the Phlegraean Fields, but it was "impossible to connect the little dirty suburb full of beggars & beggar-boatmen, & beggar-choacheys" with the ancients he revered. In the Grotto, the amusement offered was to expose a dog to the sulfurous vapor until it appeared dead, and then restore it by bringing it out—an entertainment Emerson refused to sponsor. (The same cluster of would-be guides and miserable structures surrounds the Solfatura today.)

Poverty brought out the worst in the people. Everywhere he was besieged by beggars. No ruin could be observed in peace, in open country, as he had imagined. Instead, "a vermin of ciceroni & padroni" surrounded all the antiquities he had once imagined standing freely in their solitude, "their broken columns & fallen friezes . . . solemn & eloquent."

Even the guide he hired turned out to be a notorious robber, and the diffident Emerson was embarrassed to find himself and the boy assailed by gangs of men, women, and children, all crying *"Signore, C'e un mariolo"*—"he's a thief." After the second such warning, he got rid of the questionable youth—but the next one he employed ended by demanding "three or four times his due," and evidently was unable to protect him from "one stout fellow" at the Temple of Serapis, who tried to pick his torn handkerchief from his pocket. He found the Temple of Venus, but "to what base uses turned . . . almost all standing, & even some delicate bas-reliefs remain upon the ceiling, [but it] is now a cooper's shop, & asses bray in it."

He enjoyed the museums, but he lamented the contrast between the Raphaels, Titians, Guidos, and Correggios he saw on the walls, and the indifferent work of the copiers who sat before them: "No original art remains." The people too had degenerated from the noble classical models evident in the busts of Cicero, Seneca, and the like: "Nothing is more striking than the contrast of the purity, the severity expressed in these fine old heads, with the frivolity & sensuality of the mob that exhibits & the mob that gazes at them."

At least the churches continued to hold their solace for him. The Neapolitans decorate their palaces and churches not merely on their prominent features, so to speak, but up to the eyebrows and beyond. The nave of San Martino—where Emerson stayed some time, meditating on the Guido near the altar—is one of the city's most impressive churches and a good example of its flair for ornament. Set high on a hill overlooking the city, it is so frescoed and filled with statuary that there is no corner, no awkward spot where vault meets plane, that has not been fitted with a niche and a saint, all lit by fullest daylight from the high lantern and windows. The effect is not of ostentation but of delight in abundance, as if light itself were a medium.

"Who can imagine the effect of a true & worthy form of worship in these godly piles?" Emerson asked. "It would ravish us."

DESPITE his general disappointment and frustration, however, toward the end of his stay an unexpected thing happened. "Out of the lion's mouth, honey." Naples, the nadir of his journey, also became an important turning point.

He made excursions to Vesuvius and Pompeii. The first was interesting, the second fascinating. For this extraordinary city of the dead, destroyed by Vesuvius in A.D. 92, is a vivid paradox, at once a grim waste and a living museum preserving the least details of an entire city's life that ended in minutes under the gaseous cloud and ashy blanket of the volcano. Bodies were found still crouched under the impact of this cloud, their utensils of daily life at hand, their dogs near them—all buried together and turned to stone. It seemed to him that the shops, bake-houses, halls, and court, the prison, mills, and temples he visited had not been empty twenty years. He noticed the colors of the frescoes—the reds and yellows, the richness of the marbles and beauty of the mosaics.

What enchanted him most was the overview, the sense of light and air hovering above these ruins: "I climbed a ruin which commanded a view of almost the whole excavation. The whole world has no other such view." When he visited the amphitheater outside the town

> . . . the view from its top made me wish to sit down & spend the day. Far around is this green & fertile land sprinkled plentifully with white villages & palaces, washed by the sea, adorned with islands, & close at hand on the other side the solemn mountain, author of all this ruin, & now black with recent streams of lava, without a green shrub, or so much as a blade of grass upon its side and a little smoke stealing out of the summit as if to say—The fire that once & again has ravaged this garden, is not quenched.

He read in the landscape of Pompeii and Vesuvius the same contrasting messages he had seen where Etna had loomed over the beaches of Catania: green life on the one hand, black death on the other. However disappointing his days in Naples had been, the subterranean channel that carried this dialogue onward had not been stopped, only muted. In a day or two it found new expression.

The occasion was one of the few experiences that could reliably move Emerson to anger—hearing bad preaching. "Attended service in the English Chapel," he re-

57

ported, "nothing could be more insipid, inane, than the Sermon." "The hungry sheep look up and are not fed," he had quoted from Milton when the storms at sea had been roughest. This moment, potentially so rich, here so empty, was apparently the irritant he needed to find his own voice.

A year and a half later he wrote in his journal, "Remember the Sunday morning in Naples, when I said, 'This moment is the truest vision, the best spectacle I have seen amid all the wonder and this moment, this vision, I might have had in my own closet in Boston.' " It was probably this very Sunday that he had this moment of insight, for his thought on that day continued, after criticizing the sermon, "I thought how always we are beginning to live, & how perfectly practicable at all times is the sublime part of life, the high hours, for which all the rest are given."

This was to be a recurrent theme in Emerson's thought: that a new life is always at hand, if we are able to open our eyes and gain consciousness of it. That was the great object: an accession of consciousness, an awakening of true vision. He might think he could have had this vision in his own room, his closet in Boston—but he had not. He had taken ship to Malta on an impulse, and he had been deeply right.

And so, in spite of the drenching storms, the importunate street folk, and the many eccentricities of this time-worn city, Naples became a turning point in his experience of Italy. The poem he had roughed out in Catania on March 1, he revised in Naples. Only the last lines differed from its earlier version. The changes underscored the symbolism of seeing "the morning in/such low moist roadside where blue violets peep,/magic remembrances out of the black loam." To these lines, stopped now only by a comma, he added: "Pathetic, silent poets that sing to me,/Thine elegy, sweet singer, sainted wife."

Evidently, something had been released within him. He could refer to Ellen and her death directly; he could, in effect, let her rest in the black loam. In the year before his journey, in what was apparently a classic "anniversary reaction" to her death, he had on one of his obsessive morning visits to her grave actually opened her coffin—a moment of temporary, crazed grief he recorded cryptically in his journal. Death for Emerson—surrounded as he had been by it since infancy by the premature deaths of his father, older brother, and sister—was always an extraordinarily difficult burden. But he had understood at some preconscious level, it would seem, that he must both confront it and choose away from it. This is perhaps the reason for the pattern of contrasting messages he saw in the Italian landscape. Italy—the land of empire, art, and love—Italy and the spring were working their slow miracle; Emerson was coming back to life.

~ Street in Pompeii.

ROME

"Rome fashions my dreams"

HE spent four weeks in Rome and gave it all his energy, cramming an enormous amount into each day. It repaid him, for he was intensely, if not consistently, happy throughout this special month. Rome had an important influence on his thinking, for during this visit his response to art, already awake, grew educated. New people, new experiences, and new sensibilities gave him significant insights.

Emerson hit the ground running, almost literally, when he reached Rome at last. From Naples, he traveled by coach all day and night, stopping only for meals and making haste through the Pontine marshes, notoriously infested by thieves and malaria. It was day as they passed by the fragmentary Roman aqueducts on the city's outskirts, strange lonely wrecks still visible on the flat plains, and the tomb of Cecilia Metella, famous since classical poetry and celebrated by Byron. The next day his journal, usually so loquacious, consists of a single sentence: "Rome. 27 March. It is even so; my poor feet are sore with walking all this day amongst the ruins of Rome."

Artists from the north—German and Nordic as well as Anglo-American—have had a long love affair with Rome, for its indescribable wealth of art and architecture is packed into a small, dense space, manageable in size but deep in history. The great monuments—St. Peter's, the Colosseum, the Baths of Caracalla, the Tiber itself with its many graceful, flat-arched bridges, the famous palaces and hills and columns, the ancient marketplaces, once fields where Roman soldiers trained—all lie unshadowed by the new, and the twisting dark streets beckon the wanderer with mystery, not menace.

It is a city of bright sunlight and deep shadow, of elegant oval piazzas embellished over two thousand years, and of ancient buildings like the Theater of Marcellus, seemingly a grand ruin standing between the Tiber and the Forum, but its pre-Christian walls are honeycombed by inhabited apartments that deck their windowsills with pots of red geraniums and blue shirts drying in the sun. Built into one side of the theater is a Roman temple—but the temple has become a church, and stretching up the street from its side are the houses of the most ancient ghetto, for Jews lived in Rome before there were Christians. Down the street and around the corner of the same street rise the dark, grim arches of the Palazzo Cenci. For a man with a problematic relation to history, Emerson had come to the right place.

Lodgings he found without difficulty at the Gran Bretagna in the ancient Piazza di Spagna. This quarter, located at the foot of the Pincian Hill and beside the exquisite Spanish Steps that sweep up to the Church of Trinità dei Monti, was already favored by Anglo-Americans. Just beside those steps was the severe Roman house in whose corner bedroom, overlooking the piazza, Keats had died eleven years earlier. Higher on the slope, above the church, Hawthorne later found a house and lived for two years. Emerson's own chambers cost him just fifty cents a night with evening coffee included; a three-course meal for dinner in Lepri's, the best restaurant, was only fifteen cents.

Rome in March and early April can be cold and wet. Its colors are dun, brown, gray, and black when the river Tiber is full with rain and a turbid jade in color; the sky weeps; the weather is chill. The streets are paved with black diamonds of lava, set vertically into the earth by hand and polished by eons of traffic. At that season, they shine unevenly in the rain, and the slipping foot is glad for the spaces between them.

The artist E. Roesler Franz (1845–1907), a genre painter who combined realism with a sentimental love of the antique, used this rain-dimmed light in his popular "views" of Rome. In them we see how little has changed in some sections since Emerson arrived there a hundred and fifty-odd years ago. Franz's subjects were not the grand buildings, but the structures and people of Trastevere, the oldest inhabited section of Rome: the remaining scrap of the Ponte Rotto, or a peasant woman, white blouse set off by her crimson skirts, a great bundle of wash on her head, standing at the corner of a suitably dilapidated piazza, or a raffish muleteer atop his red-wheeled cart that overwhelms the little donkey that draws it along the cobbled street. Young Julian Hawthorne, then about twelve, saw similar figures when he roamed about the city—in fact, he watched one such woman stab and kill a man who had insulted her and then walk calmly away through the parting crowd; Romans, the boy understood, respected her defense of her honor.*

*Julian Hawthorne, *Hawthorne and His Circle* (New York: Archon Books, 1968), 306–308.

But Emerson, though he would have seen these things, was not in search of charm. What he wanted was not the picturesque, conceived in nostalgia and born old, but the sublime: visions, episodes, spectacles that would stir him to the depths and make him aware of what the universe was about. In Rome, he was in the center of the center. If he could not find it here, it did not exist.

Fortunately, by now he had met a number of traveling Americans, mostly Harvard graduates and friends of his brothers Charles and Edward. The group changed as its members came and left the city, but he now had people with whom to dine and walk, and in consequence Rome became "very pleasant to me, as Naples was not."

Emerson arrived in time for Easter and its impressive celebrations, the preferred season for visiting Rome, and he made St. Peter's his first destination. In the next eight or ten hours, he covered the city almost from one end to the other, crossing and recrossing the Tiber as he took in Raphael's frescoes, the "FORUM," the Tarpeian Rock, the house of Rienzi, celebrated by Byron, the Capitoline Hill and its museums; then he turned around and retraced his steps to the great cathedral, probably for vespers. Rome lay all before him, but only for four weeks, and he was determined to let none of it escape.

Gradually, however, his pace slowed as his sense of his own taste developed. He visited and studied the major ruins, but as he wrote, "In Rome all is ruinous. In the garden before my window the flowerpots stand upon blocks made of the capitals of old columns, turned upside down." Carved stones that once ornamented mansions and temples were now used as rubble to fill a wall. Archaeological Roman history, however, was only of moderate interest to him. He was gifted with acute visual sensitivity, and he was dazzled by the art. The "vast & splendid Vatican Museum" he called "a wilderness of marble." He had seen casts of the famous sculptures, and was ready to like the originals, but he could not have imagined the total experience:

On we went from chamber to chamber through galleries of statues & vases & sarcophagi & bas reliefs & busts & candelabra—through all forms of beauty & richest materials—till the eye was dazzled & glutted with this triumph of the arts. Go and see it, whoever you are. It is the wealth of the civilized world.

But the painting that his era had been taught by Sir Joshua Reynolds to prize above all others, Raphael's *Transfiguration*, lay ahead, and Emerson was prepared.

63

Much will have more. We knew that the first picture in the world was in the same house & we left all this pomp to go & see the Transfiguration by Raphael.

It was conventional to admire extravagantly this painting by Raphael, but it is a powerful masterwork in spite of our twentieth-century prejudice against hyperbole. It did not disappoint Emerson. Its "calm benignant beauty seems almost to call you by name," he said, giving it his highest accolade: an awakened sense of kinship with genius. He ranked the artist with "the first born of the earth," but said he found Christ's "sweet and sublime" face a "familiar simple homespeaking countenance."

There was an established canon of important works which Anglo-American visitors made sure to see: *The Dying Gladiator*, as it was then called, *The Laocoön*, various works by Raphael (his paintings of his mistress, occasionally half-clad, caused some tut-tutting, however), and anything by Michelangelo.* Guido Reni, known as Guido, was especially praised, and his painting of a young girl in the Barberini Palace, commonly supposed to be Beatrice Cenci, was sought out for meditation. (Hawthorne incorporated this work and its grim subtext into his novel *The Marble Faun*.) Sight-seers had an easier time then than today, for the pre-Raphaelite painters had not yet been rediscovered. Titian and Tintoretto might be studied; some of the late-seventeenth-century French artists such as Lorrain and Poussin as well. But Fra Angelico, Giotto, Uccello, even Botticelli—not to mention the primitives—were virtually unknown to the educated public.

About some of the young Americans, Emerson had misgivings: "Alas for the young men that come here & walk in Rome without one Roman thought! They unlearn their English & their morals, & violate the sad solitude of the mother of nations." He meant vulgarity of mind and not only sexuality: "They think the Coliseum [*sic*] is a very *nice* place."

Yet Emerson spent most of his time with the young artists he had met, although some seemed too young and "green." It was a matter of choice. He was dispassionate but sympathetic toward the risks of their undertaking:

What is more pathetic than the Studio of a young Artist? No rags & disease in the street move you to sadness like the lonely chamber littered round with sketches & canvases & colourbags. There is something so gay in the art itself that these rough & poor commencements contrast more painfully with it. Here another enthusiast feeds himself with hope & rejoices in dreams & smarts with mortifications. The melancholy artist told me that if the end of painting was to please the eye, he would throw away his pallet [*sic*]. And yet how many of them not only fail to reach the soul with their conceptions, but fail to please the eye.

*Paul Baker, *The Fortunate Pilgrims: Americans in Italy 1800–1860* (Cambridge, Mass.: Harvard University Press, 1964), 125 and chapter 6 passim.

~ *The Dying Gaul, Capitoline Museum. "The dying Gladiator is a most expressive statue but it will always be indebted to the muse of Byron for fixing upon it forever his pathetic thought."*

~ Capitoline Museum, Hall of Philosophers, Rome.

~ Room of the Emperors, Capitoline Museum. *"It is a grand town, & works mightily upon the senses & upon the soul. It fashions my dreams even, & all night I visit Vaticans" (opposite).*

In this anonymous young man Emerson recognized, consciously or not, a kindred Romantic spirit striving to "reach the soul" with his work. It was not this artist's aim but his talent that he doubted.

It is significant that Emerson, the straitlaced if renegade minister, was more comfortable with young, creative artists than with his social equivalents. He could just as easily have thrown in his lot with respectable folk like the Holbrooks, but he had reacted strongly against their pettiness and ignorance. He wrote his aunt in April of feeling "excluded from good company and yoked with green dull pitiful persons . . . cabined up by sea and by land since I left home with various little people, all better to be sure & much wiser than me but still such as did not help me." That he was alluding to the Holbrooks and Kettell is evident from the comment he made on the voyage home in September *1833*: "This time I have not drawn the golden lot of company. And yet better far than the last voyage." There was no lack of such tedious bores. "One day," he told his brother William in April, "I counted *15* persons here from Boston."

He had found their antidote, however, in the young artists he was meeting. After this starvation, "I cannot tell you how refreshing it was," his letter to his aunt continued, "to fall in with two or three sensible persons with whom I could eat my bread & take my walk & feel myself a freeman once more of God's universe." The reason behind this evident passion was that his own metamorphosis in Italy—like Goethe's before him—was taking him in their direction, toward a greater sense of his own liberty and freedom of self-expression. He might live chastely and spend his evenings alone reading Goethe and Sismondi, but he was intellectually unshackling himself. He apparently expressed his new ideas more distinctly and openly now, for in addition to the criticism in his letter to his aunt, his conversation could shock conventional people. One of these was Thomas Stewardson, a Philadelphian who was "greatly startled at Emerson's pantheistic utterances," as W.S.W. Ruschenberger notes in *A Sketch in the Life of Thomas Stewardson, M.D.* (Philadelphia, *1833*).

It is unlikely that Emerson had tried to unsettle Stewardson's views. But while his outer habits and manner remained what they had been, gradually, "a freeman once more of God's universe," he was changing, not by sloughing off a skin, but as a tree grows, beneath the bark, adding new layers of experience and strength. Clearly, that crucial sense of freedom, so different from the anxious swagger of the January

69

~ *Moses* by Michelangelo, San Pietro in Vincoli, Rome. *"Yesterday afternoon I went to the Church of S. Pietro in Vinculo to see Michel Angelo's statue of Moses. What a wonder it is! It is as great as the Greeks without reminding you of them. It is the Jewish Law embodied in a man."*

crossing, had grown in Rome in the environment of art and creative effort he found there.

THE Vatican and the Capitoline museums were each open two days a week, and with his new friends "our due feet never fail," Emerson wrote, to make the pilgrimage. Two works in particular caught his eye that were not on the syllabus. One was *The Vision of San Romoaldo* by Andreas Sacchi, in the Vatican.

> What a majestic form is the last Carmelite in the train who ascends the steps. One is greater for knowing that such forms can be. What a cant of the head has this same figure. Look at him!

That painting (praised by Reynolds) is interesting for the peculiarly intent and open expression on the face of the white-robed monk who is seated at the bottom left and appears to be listening hard and meditating deeply; even his body seems receptive to what he is experiencing.

Another work on which Emerson commented was

> . . . the beautiful head of the Justice who sits with Prudence on the monument of Paulus III on the left of the Tribuna in St. Peter's. It was designed by Michel Angelo, executed by William de la Porta, but where in the Universe is the Archetype from which the Artist drew this sweetness & grace? There is a heaven.

Interestingly, all the images Emerson singled out for praise share an expression of inwardness: a gentle detachment from surrounding circumstances, as if the subject were dwelling on and protecting something valuable. Raphael's Christ looks not down at his worshippers, but ahead and to one side, so that it is he as much as the human beings who is transfigured by his own light. The same meditation on something beyond words is in the "cant of the head" of St. Romoaldo and in the withdrawn beauty of the sculptured face on Pope Paul III's tomb.*

TO this total immersion in art Emerson responded with tremendous excitement. He was twenty-nine years old, but he had seen nothing like what burst upon him in Rome. In that era no one in America had significant firsthand acquaintance with the visual arts unless he or she traveled abroad. There were casts of sculpture, but

*Emerson's references here are faulty. The figure who listens with canted head is seated, not standing, in Sacchi's painting, and it is Prudence who is beautiful in de la Porta's sculpture; Justice, who sits opposite her, looks grim and world-weary.

~ *Esquiline Venus*, Palazzo dei Conservatori.

photography and lithography were still in their infancy, copies of paintings were rare and museums rarer still; native art was immature.

"I lie down at night enriched by the contemplation of great objects," he wrote his brother Charles in April. "It is a grand town, & works mightily upon the senses and upon the soul. It fashions my dreams even, & all night I visit Vaticans." This was no exaggeration. He reported the same thing in his journal: "Rome fashions my dreams. All night I wander amidst statues & fountains, and last night was introduced to Lord Byron!" Byron had been the hero of his youthful desire to be a poet himself, and to dream that he met him on his own grounds—for Byron had loved Rome— suggests how enlarged Emerson felt by his new experience.

That sense of growth is evident also in the comment that opened the same letter: "We grow wiser by the day, & by the hour." The gnawing sense of emptiness Emerson sometimes felt was here assuaged, at least in part: "Ah great great Rome!" he wrote, "It is a majestic city, & satisfies this craving imagination."

It is less of a paradox than it seems that, in the same letter, immediately he added, "And yet I would give all Rome for one man such as were fit to walk here, & could feel & impart the sentiment of the place. That wise man whom every where I seek, here I hunger & thirst after." That he was not lonely in the literal sense, Emerson hastened to add, mentioning his pleasant companionship.

What he yearned for, "that wise man whom every where I seek," was no ordinary other, clearly, but a teacher, a friend of the deepest sort, an interlocutor of the soul. Emerson's consciousness of this need, however, implies not a true deficit but a sort of overflowing. He had begun to feel at home in the city; he had his bearings. What he needed now was someone with whom to articulate and to whom he could impart what he, "wiser by the day, & by the hour," was accumulating. Perhaps he was realizing that in order to find "the Man" he wanted, he must become him.

Emerson spent a good deal of his time in the precincts of St. Peter's, but he began with a normal Protestant distrust of Catholic ceremonies, which he at first dismissed as "millinery & imbecility." His thought evolved from that position quickly, however. The music of the *Miserere*, sung at vespers in the Sistine Chapel, especially moved him, and with repeated visits he began to feel the point of the dramatic liturgy:

> . . . All the candles in the chapel are extinguished but one . . . then out of the silence & the darkness rises this most plaintive & melodious strain, "Miserere me, Deus" . . . these forms strike me more than I expected.

On a subsequent evening he watched the long religious procession move through part of the cathedral:

~ *Socrates,* Hall of Philosophers, Capitoline Museum. *"That wise man whom everywhere I seek, here I hunger & thirst after."*

. . . You walk about on its ample marble pavement as you would on a common, so free are you of your neighbors . . . [and amid the] mighty gilded arches & vaults & far windows & brave columns [its] rich clad priests . . . look as if they were the pictures come down from the walls & walking.

He reported Pope Gregory XVI to be "a learned & able man; he was a monk & is reputed of pure life." Emerson would not have been Emerson if he had not wished the head of the world's most hierarchical church would leave "this formal service of fifty generations & speak out of his own heart." But his objections were increasingly *pro forma*, and he made a similar but harsher criticism of "divine service at the English Chapel" the next week. "To preach well you must speak the truth. It is vain to say what has been said every Sunday for a hundred years, if it is not true."

By the end of Easter week he had gone from saying "There is no true majesty in all this millinery & imbecility," to the assertion that Pope Gregory's public Easter blessing was a "sublime spectacle," and the simple admission, "I love St Peter's Church. It grieves me that after a few days I shall see it no more. . . . It is an ornament of the earth. It is not grand, it is so rich & pleasing; it should rather be called the sublime of the beautiful."

Rome, in short, had enlarged Emerson in ways he could not have anticipated, and quite as much as he could have hoped. The very hunger he felt for deeper company than "green dull pitiful persons" was a sign of his growth. Unlike Montaigne, he had held no learned disputes with prelates of the office of the Inquisition; unlike Byron, he had engaged in no Roman dalliances. But he had shed his unhappiness and much of his self-doubt along with his ill health. He wrote his aunt in a letter, quoted above:

Did they tell you I went away from home a wasted peevish invalid. Well I have been mending ever since & am now in better health than I remember to have enjoyed since I was in college. How should one be sick at Rome? It is a wonderful town.

In this wonderful town, "great great Rome"—he had begun to grow wings. The next stage of his journey—up the Tiber and its tributaries to Florence—would find him fully fledged.

~ Monument to Alexander VII by Bernini, St. Peter's, Rome.

TUSCANY

"Why should painters study at Rome? Here, here."

FLORENCE lay five and a half days north through the soft hills and fertile plains of Umbria and Tuscany. Emerson took the ancient via Flaminia north to Terni, birthplace of Tacitus, with its great cascade, and then continued up the valley of the Tessina past Spoleto, Foligno, Assisi, and Perugia. Many of these places had been celebrated by Byron, whose spirit haunted them for Emerson, and some by Horace also, like the little Temple of Clitumnus near Assisi. Emerson remembered here that Byron had written of its "small and delicate proportions." Now it has sunk below the road and is shrouded in scaffolding, but the little roof and columns still look up unexpectedly only a few feet from the silently welling stream where Horace said, "white oxen bathe."*

Spoleto, too, he noted, was a town beloved by St. Francis for its austere, medieval beauty. It perches like an eagle on its hilltop, crowned by the great fortress of La Rocca and eyeing the opposite hill to which it is tethered by an elegant aqueduct, *700* feet wide and *300* feet high, first built by the Romans.

It was a peaceful journey that gave Emerson time to reflect. North of Rome at that season the brown hills are streaked vertically with green, as if someone had wiped her paintbrush, and the sun and clouds chase each other across a windy sky. Tuscany drapes her vineyards across her flanks like scarves, and the landscape expresses a timeless peace.

HE was to spend four weeks in Florence, and by the time he arrived in early May, Emerson was composed in mind and ready to be pleased. He no longer felt like a

*Gilbert Highet, *Poets in a Landscape* (New York: Knopf, *1957*), *88, 106*.

nomad, surprised to find himself in the world's center. His tone was that of a civilized man of the world, able to make informed comparisons:

> And how do you like Florence? Why, well. It is pleasant to see how affectionately all the artists who have resided here a little while speak of getting home to Florence. And I found at once that we live here with much more comfort than in Rome or Naples. Good streets, industrious population, spacious well furnished lodgings, elegant & cheap Caffès, the cathedral & the Campanile, the splendid galleries and no beggars—make this city the favorite of strangers.

Emerson was right about this preference, especially among the Anglo-Americans. Less heterogeneous than Rome, younger in age and more unified in style, Florence, child of the Renaissance, has a chaste severity in its lines and a golden aura in its color that make it very different from its southern sister. It is Botticelli, not Raphael; Donatello, not Bernini. Spreading away from the placid Arno, the whole city can be taken in at a glance from the hill of the Boboli Gardens: in the middle, Brunelleschi's magnificent red-tiled dome soars over the cathedral; around it lie the right-angled roofs of the palaces; to the left rise the towers of Santa Maria Novella, near which Emerson stayed. Wide bridges supported on rhythmic, harmonious arches cross the green-brown Arno, which glints in the sunlight through the arcades of the old bridge, the Ponte Vecchio, and its double row of goldsmiths' shops.

He and one of the artists he had met in Rome soon fell in with other Americans, and by the time he left Florence they had formed a traveling group that consisted of themselves and Thomas Stewardson of Philadelphia. Two women, Miss Anna Bridgen of Albany and her sister, ladies he had already met in Rome, were also companions. Eventually they were all to travel together on their journey north.

EMERSON had gained more than a sophisticated tone by this point. In the south in February he had observed the spring with delight mixed with sadness. Three months later he was more open to purely sensuous delight. The weather had turned hot almost as soon as he arrived, so hot, the Florentines told him, "there is nobody but dogs and Englishmen in the streets." Emerson had probably adopted the habit of the siesta by now, for not only were most places shut during the afternoon heat, but he was taking his walks in the cool hours of the day: in the evening between six and eight, or in the early morning, strolling along the beautiful esplanades beside the Arno or in the Boboli Gardens.

~ Vicolo della Basilica, Spoleto. *"All the streets of this town have been shaken by earthquakes; the houses lean, and are kept from falling by timbers which cross the street from house to house."*

~ Ponte delle Torri, Spoleto. *"Here too was a prodigious aqueduct 300 feet high."*

~ Detail of façade, San Pietro, Spoleto.

~ San Salvatore, Spoleto.

~ Landscape near Castiglione, Umbria.

~ Monastery of San Damiano, Assisi.

~ Basilica of San Francesco, Assisi.

And wherever I go, I am surrounded by these beautiful objects; the fine old towers of the city; the elegant curve of the Ponte Trinità; the rich purple line of the Appenines [*sic*]; broken by the bolder summits of the marble mountains of Carrara. And all all is Italian; not a house, not a shed, not a field that the eye can for a moment imagine to be American.

On another day he rose early and went to Bellosguardo, a hilltop village southwest of the city. "It was a fine picture this Tuscan morning and all the towers of Florence rose richly out of the smoky light on the broad green plain."

He was in rhythm with the life around him—the weather, the climate, the curves of bridge and mountain range—and he was tasting all that was Italian and Tuscan with intense awareness of its flavor. To know each better was also a step in his education of the self. He had not given up his capacity for judgment (as his allusion to anecdotes about the depravity of morals in Florence suggests), but he was more able to yield himself to enjoyment. The embarrassments of traveling had diminished; he was a more accomplished man, and a happier one.

His sense of himself as a social creature was also developing. He realized this after a few weeks when he wrote in May to his friend George Sampson that "it is necessary in order to see what is worth seeing & especially *who* is worth seeing in each city, to go a little into society," an insight he repeated in his journal next day. Evidently it was a new thought, though he was only five days short of his thirtieth birthday. For an avowed bookworm, this was real progress.

Consequently, he made more calls on society in Florence than in all his previous traveling, visiting Henry Miles, an American merchant, Professor Amici, famous maker of astronomical instruments, Horatio Greenough, considered the most talented sculptor working in Italy, and others. He also attended the opera four times, having at last heard a singer, Sgra. Delsere, whom he found moving and worthy of respect (on other occasions he had decided the experience was not worthwhile). He liked the production, but not the inflated acting style of the other performers: "Everything good but the strutting of the actors. Is it penal for an actor to *walk*?" He credited Goethe with teaching him to be openminded and transcend his prejudices against displays of sensual material. Nevertheless, it was sometimes more than his "Puritan starch" could stand, and God was clearly on his side: "I have since learned God's decision on the same, in the fact that all the *ballerine* are nearly ideotic [*sic*]." (He also deplored something else in a single, unexplained phrase: "But the *boys*.")

It took no act of transcendence to appreciate the human charm of Erminia, the flower girl, of whom he left a portrait:

I met the fair Erminia today. These meetings always cost me a crazie and it is fit that she should not be slighted in the journal. Erminia is a flower-girl who comes to the Caffé every morning & if you will not buy her flowers she gives them to you & with such a superb air. She has a fine expression of face & never lets her customers pass her in the street without a greeting. Every coach too in Florence that ventures to stop near the Piazza di Trinita is a tributary of Erminia's. I defy them to escape from her nosegays. She has a rich pearl necklace worth I know not how much, which she wears on festas. Mr. Wall wishes to paint her portrait but she says she is not handsome enough. "E brutto il mio ritratto." [It would be ugly, my portrait.]

He was seeing the world, this Bostonian widower-clergyman, whose upbringing had certainly excluded operas (much less the ballet) and whose college had locked its young men in at nights rather than have them stray into the fleshpots of the town.

More to the point, he paid three calls in quick succession on the poet, Walter Savage Landor, who welcomed him to his beautiful villa on the hill of Fiesole above Florence. This was Emerson's first encounter with an English literary man, "very much a connoisseur of paintings," and a good preparation for his comical meetings later with the aged Wordsworth and Coleridge who were to lecture him, or declaim their poetry, but never to take seriously their visitor's differing views.

Landor had decided ideas on a great many subjects. Evidently they got on well, but clearly Emerson took the measure of the man who glorified Lord Chesterfield and undervalued Socrates. "He would not praise . . . my Carlyle," Emerson reported in his journal. "He pestered me with Southey; what is Southey?" Julius Hare, an English clergyman and High Churchman, was also there, and he confided to Emerson later that the learned Mr. Landor "has not more than twelve books in his library." Greenough, who accompanied Emerson on a subsequent visit and had been instrumental in introducing him, remarked that Landor, "in common with all collectors, imagines that his are the only masterpieces." (Eight years later, still offended by Landor's deliberately "cold and gratuitous" use of licentious language, Emerson published a biting impression of him in the essay "Walter Savage Landor": "Before a well-dressed company he plunges his fingers into a cesspool, as if to expose the whiteness of his hands and the jewels of his ring. Afterward, he washes them in water, he washes them in wine; but you are never secure from his freaks.")

However, it was only from meetings like these that Emerson would learn better how to judge men, their opinions, and reputations, and when he did, he concluded that it was best not to be overawed by them.

. . .

89

FOR all the extension of himself in the social sphere, it was Florence's art that provided him with his deepest experience. His first response to the city was lyrical: "How like an archangel's tent is this great Cathedral of many-coloured marble set down in the midst of the city and by its side its wondrous campanile."

In the Uffizi Gallery he was enchanted by the Medici *Venus*, " 'dazzled & drunk with beauty' " he said of himself, quoting Byron. "I think no man has an idea of the powers of painting until he has come hither. Why should painters study at Rome? Here, here."*

The architecture of the early Renaissance, however, took him longer to understand. Having begun at "the little end of Europe," and worked upward, Emerson's eye had been nourished by the Baroque and, as he knew, that "eye [had] not yet learned why" it should love the more austere style of Florence. On his first explorations inside the cathedrals, therefore, he was disappointed by the interiors, which he found "bare and poor"; he yearned for St. Peters. He wondered why Michelangelo had called Santa Maria Novella "his *bride*"; to Emerson it looked unfinished.

As a preaching order, the Franciscans have always designed their basilicas with majestic open areas where large numbers of people can gather and sound is clear; in consequence, they seem austere at first. In this as in other things, Emerson learned quickly, and when he made a second visit two weeks later to Santa Croce he recanted: "If I spoke ill of it before I will unsay it all. It is a grand building."

The great building stands on the ruins of a pagan temple, and on its broad piazza after the market closes, children play in the afternoon till dusk, as they have for the last two thousand years. Inside, the vaulted cloisters lead one into another, till the last, designed by Brunelleschi, is reached: a place of great serenity, over whose low, arcaded walls the gradually softening sky rests quietly, the light broken only by the flutter of nesting swifts. Emerson was in time for vespers and heard the organ as they were walking up and down: "I have never heard a more pleasing one."

An insight came to him at this moment that shows the increased measure of his vision:

When I walk up the piazza of Santa Croce I feel as if it were not a Florentine nor an European church but a church built by & for the human race. I feel equally at home within its walls as the Grand duke, so *hospitably* sound to me the names of its mighty dead. Buonaroti & Galileo lived for us all.

*We gaze and turn away, and know not where, Dazzled and drunk with beauty, till the heart Reels with its fulness; there—for ever there— Chain'd to the chariot of triumphal Art, We stand as captives, and would not depart. [Childe Harold, 49–50]

This Roman Catholic church in all its beauty was built "for the human race"—as much for him as for anyone else. The names of the mighty dead entombed within it sounded "hospitably" in his ears because they had "lived for us all." The phrases are significant. We take such ecumenicism today for granted, but it was rare and new in that era—and new for Emerson, as well. The man who could not serve Communion because it had become an empty, repugnant rite was regaining in these moments his grasp on the language and meaning of communal experience; at this instant in Santa Croce he shared experience that enlarged him vicariously (they "lived for us all") and enabled him to feel his kinship with other great souls as mystery, not mythology. If he had gained nothing further from his voyage than this, perhaps it would have been enough.

EMERSON'S month in Florence, though less intense than the one in Rome, was probably more comfortable. It was a period of ripening and consolidation, when the new experiences in which he had been immersed all spring had been absorbed and were producing new growth. Occasionally even in Rome he had still felt he would like to hide himself in a "thicket," so chagrined was he at his occasional gaucherie. But by the end of May, those days were behind him. He had companionship, a better command of Italian, and knowledge of art and the country. The "growth of the true self," the vision that felt itself a "freeman . . . of God's universe" were become realities.

On the twenty-eighth of the month, three days after his thirtieth birthday, he and his friends climbed into their *vettura* and turned northward once more. In two weeks of steady travel, their voyage in Italy would be over.

~ Duomo, Florence. *"How like an archangel's tent is this great Cathedral of many coloured marble set down in the midst of the city and by its side its wondrous campanile!"*

~ Ponte Trinità, Florence.

Preceding pages:

~ Boboli Gardens, Florence *(left).*

~ Cloister by Brunelleschi, Santa Croce, Florence.
"I feel . . . at home within its walls" (right).

~ Florence from the Piazzale Michelangelo.
*"Rose early this morng. & went to the Bello
Sguardo out of the Roman gate. It was a fine
picture this Tuscan morning and all the towers
of Florence rose richly out of the smoky light
on the broad green plain."*

THE NORTH

THE last leg of Emerson's trip took him through nine major cities of northern Italy in fifteen days, an arduous route northeast through the mountains and over the plains to Venice, and then west again to Milan and the Alps. He was sustained by his desire to conclude the trip, and the change of pace was probably welcome.

There were significant moments, although nothing could equal the revelations of Rome and Florence. At the foot of the green Euganean Hills, almost in sight of Venice, he sent the carriage ahead and climbed up to visit Petrarch's last home. In the austere, fourteenth-century villa, surrounded by a walled garden and looking out into the hills, the great poet and statesman had spent his last years. Emerson was moved by its tranquillity: "Good good place. It does honor to his head & heart; there grow the pomegranate & fig & olive."

Ferrara appealed to his sense of pathos. There he visited the dark cellar where the poet Tasso had been imprisoned on the pretext of madness by Alfonso, one of the cruelest of the Dukes of Este, whom Byron had made famous with the malediction he wrote on the spot:

> On Tasso's name attend
> The tears and praises of all time; while thine
> Would rot in its oblivion—in the sink
> Of worthless dust. . . .
> . . . but the link
> Thou formest in his fortunes bids us think
> Of thy poor malice, naming thee with scorn. . . .
> [Childe Harold, 36–37]

99

"Italy is Byron's debtor," Emerson had written in Rome, "and I think no one knows how fine a poet he is who has not seen the subjects of his verse." As if the city suffered under a curse, grass grew in its streets; it was "a desolate town," and in traversing it he saw with indignation the ghetto, "the Jews' quarters of whom there are *2800* who are shut up every night as in Rome like dogs."

Nearby was Padua, where his sharp eye, by now well educated, picked up an image of the furnishings in the beautiful—and then new—Caffè Pedrocchi, "the most beautiful Caffe in Europe." (It is still charming.) It was a revelation to him of the new Empire style, and when a few days later he saw Canova's famous statue of Pauline Bonaparte in Venice, he recognized that "the chair in which he has seated [her] is the same beautiful form I admired in the Caffe."

After the first day, Venice, the object of the northeast leg, did not appeal to him. His first impression of St. Mark's under the full moon was that it "was all glorious to behold . . . this arabesque square is all enchantment—so rich & strange & vision-ary." But he soon found something inimical in the very idea of the city. It was too wet and too crowded. "You are always in a gutter. . . . I am speedily satisfied with Venice. It is a great oddity—a city for beavers . . . a most disagreeable residence. You feel always in prison, & solitary." No place but on St. Mark's piazza was there enough room for a thousand men to find elbow room, and the gondolas, though luxurious, cut off human intercourse. Moreover, "there is always a slight smell of bilgewater about the thing, & houses in the water remind me of a freshet & desola-tion. . . . I soon had enough of it."

The scale of the paintings and the splendor of the churches were admirable, but he decided he still preferred Raphael to Titian. Moreover, everything he visited was shadowed for him by the horrors of its more recent history, for Venice had become a byword for cruel and corrupt government. Emerson was sickened when the guides displayed the prisons and instruments of torture and glad that the Venetian govern-ment had been conquered by the French and Austrians.

THERE was one city of importance left to see, and four days after leaving Venice Emerson reached Milan "by a broad and splendid street." Everything that was odd and Byzantine was left behind: Milan has long been a thriving city, its magnificent Gothic monuments living comfortably on in a modern setting, and for once in this country Emerson was struck more by its charity—the Ospitale Grande, a free hospi-tal with *2,500* beds—than by its beggary.

By now he was an accomplished, if not weary, traveler. "We have 'killed it thoroughly,' " he reported of Milan in his best tourist's style after seeing eight churches and all the curiosities of the town in a single day—aided by the Comte del Verme and the use of his coach.

They had also visited the cathedral, one of the glories of Milan and of Italy. Begun in the fourteenth century, it was "not yet finished though always being built." After long years of neglect, it is today almost completely cleaned, scrubbed so that its white marble again gleams as it did when Emerson saw it. He was enchanted, commenting on its five thousand existing statues, the two thousand still planned, and the forty-two artists perpetually employed upon it. The only truly Gothic cathedral he had seen in Italy, it is famous for its glass as well as its noble proportions. The east windows especially impressed him. "These huge windows contain the whole history of Mankind from Adam & Eve down, each pane being a separate picture."

What he liked best, however, was the roof, an air-garden made of stone, broad enough to walk on amid "scores of exquisitely sculptured pinnacles rising & flowering all around you, the noble city of Milan beneath, and all the Alps in the horizon,—it is one of the grandest views on earth."

That visit was characteristic of Emerson. He had a liking for high places, and wherever he went he would find some bell tower, or promontory, or rock, or cupola, or pinnacle, and there perch and consider the world. In Sicily he had made a detour to mount that place for goats, Taormina; in Palermo he had climbed on foot to Monreale. At Naples he ascended the Vomero, and went higher yet to the terrace beside San Martino to hear the *400,000* voices noisily coming up to meet him—and then had found peace sitting at the highest point above Pompeii. He had not failed to mount Vesuvius. Rome had furnished him with plenty of hills and views, the best of which had been his climb into the cupola atop St. Peter's, no trivial feat, for it involves hundreds of slippery marble steps ascending in spirals and much gripping of sloping walls, before the city and plains of the Roman countryside are spread out below one's feet and the wind whistles in one's ears. Undoubtedly, he had climbed the exquisite bell tower Giotto designed for Florence, for he also mounted the campanile in Venice and compared it unfavorably to the other.

But his most idiosyncratic ascent took place in the hill town of Pratolino, situated high on a ridge just outside of Florence. To the northwest the high peaks of the Apennines rise *6,000* to *7,000* feet, sloping northeast toward Bologna. Looking out at these mountains in Pratolino in what is now the Villa Demidoff is John of Bologna's colossal hollow statue known by Emerson as "Father Appenine [*sic*]"—a figure Montaigne had seen when it was being built. Emerson reported, "Stopped at the Pratolino five miles out of the city to see the colossal statue of Father Appenine [*sic*].

~ Palazzo dei Diamanti, Ferrara *(opposite)*.

~ Castello d'Este, Ferrara. *"Visited Tasso's prison, a real dungeon. . . . The guide said his father accompanied him & that Byron staid an hour & a half in the prison & there wrote."* Byron's attack on Alfonso's cruelty made this Duke of Este infamous:

> *On Tasso's name attend*
> *The tears and praises of all time; while thine*
> *Would rot in its oblivion—in the sink*
> *Of worthless dust. . . .*
> *. . . but the link*
> *Thou formest in his fortunes bids us think*
> *Of thy poor malice, naming thee with scorn. . . .*
> [Childe Harold, *IV, 36–37*]

~ Petrarch's Chair, Arqua Petrarca.

~ Page of the Visitor's Book with Byron's signature, Petrarch's villa in Arqua Petrarca. *"Italy is Byron's debtor, and I think no one knows how fine a poet he is who has not seen the subjects of his verse."*

It is grand if only from its size. . . . I got up into his neck & looked out of his ear. Fine mountain scenery to the frontier of the Roman state."

It is an odd phrase—"got up into his neck & looked out of his ear"—and an odd moment, its quirkiness captured by his language. One could call it an example of traveler's synesthesia, sought for the same reason as the poetic kind, to heighten and intensify experience. But it is also an image of Gulliver in Brobdingnag, the land of the giants.

It was not the first time Emerson had put himself in that position. Even his visit to Petrarch's home in the Euganean Hills he had made voluntarily into an uphill climb, sending the carriage ahead on the plain and mounting the steep hill on foot, as if on a pilgrimage. Climbing up and looking out were what his trip had been about, after all, from first to last. Only in that way could he measure himself. Only from such a vantage point could he hope to glimpse what he needed to see. Near Florence he looked at the Apennines; in Milan he strained for sight of the Alps. He sought the sublime, and where the border was, where the mountains rose in their heights to meet the sky was always the spot Emerson wished to fix upon.

He had not yet finished his trip in the literal sense when he left Milan and crossed the same Alps. Paris (which he generally disliked) lay ahead; after that, six weeks in England and Scotland would provide him with a sense of that country and a meeting with Carlyle, whom he was long to value as a friend. There he also met the aged Coleridge and Wordsworth, no mean achievements, but hardly meaningful encounters. He had come to Europe probably hoping that through contact with its great creative men he would also encounter what was highest in human nature. If so, he was surely disappointed. He wanted them to be great souls, but the Coleridge who met him wore "goggles" and—himself once a Unitarian—lectured him against his denomination, while Wordsworth had chatted about trivia: "Could not Wordsworth have kept to himself," Emerson wondered while waiting to sail home in September, "his intimations that his new edition was at the bookseller's & contained some improvements? John Milton was a poet not a bookmaker. . . ."

He thanked God for having led him through

this European scene, this last schoolroom. . . . He has shown me the men I wished to see—Landor, Coleridge, Carlyle, Wordsworth—he has thereby comforted & confirmed me in my convictions. Many things I owe to the sight of these men. I shall judge more justly, less timidly, of wise men forevermore. To be sure not one of these is a mind of the very first class . . . they never *fill the ear*—fill the mind.

106

To one who did not know them by reputation, they would seem only "sensible well read earnest men—not more." And especially all of them were deficient—and he included Carlyle—"in insight into religious truth."

THE glimpse of the sublime, the "wise man whom every where I seek" would not be found in other men. And if it rested at the horizon, it was at the horizon of the mind, not of the senses. That much he knew by the time he took ship in Liverpool harbor to return to the United States. He was at sea on a day of fair fine wind, out of sight of land, when he took up his journal and made his first reference to the book that would make him famous: "I like my book about nature & wish I knew where & how I ought to live. God will show me." He said no more of it until he was engrossed in its writing.

"My book about nature"—the phrase is so short and flat one could pass it by without notice, but it said enough. He had gone out "a peppercorn," aching to burst the bonds that enclosed his "true self." He was coming home holding tight within himself the seed of a book, *Nature*, that was to change his life and the course of American thought. We cannot precisely apportion responsibility for the conception of that idea among countries, or persons, or other men in such matters. But Emerson spent five months traveling south of the Alps, four of them in Italy proper, and only six weeks in England. And what he was exposed to in Italy, above all, was the idea of beauty, rich and open, natural and fashioned by art, as he had never seen it before. It affected his way of thinking and his way of seeing. "Look for me under your bootsoles," Whitman wrote in ending *Leaves of Grass*. Italy similarly dissolved itself into Emerson's thought, and it has in consequence been too little seen as a crucial part of his development. He came out from Boston at a low point in his life, looking as if he would not survive the voyage. He was sustained by the ardor of his wish for an enlarged and more open vision, able, to use Wordsworth's language, to see into the heart of things, and a voice able to affirm that insight. In Italy, he was able to let go of the past and come back to life and health. As he went, he grew conscious of his message.

He profited, especially in Rome and Florence, from the examples of those creative geniuses who had left behind works of art that spoke to him across the centuries—and told him that he shared in them by understanding them, told him that he was no stranger, but a brother, another creator, hospitably welcome to the ground they consecrated. "One must be an inventor to read well," Emerson wrote a few years later in "The American Scholar." "There is, then, creative reading as well as creative writing." In Italy, he learned how good a reader he really was, and how wide were the fields of perception.

There, too, he spent months in the company of other American artists, equally obscure but equally hopeful, among whom he recognized his state of freedom. It is no accident that the images he admired most in Rome all suggest an inward brooding on and protection of a vision of beauty.

In short, the ground for his own creative breakthrough was prepared in Italy; the sense of possibility flooded in. He saw, as he had hoped to, "the utmost that man can do" (an expression he would have found in Goethe). Conversely, the scorn he felt for Landor reflected his recognition of how little depth there might be behind a grand reputation, and as he traveled later through England the anxiety at not measuring up to the highest standard continued to diminish as he observed how fundamentally ordinary even genuinely great writers might be.

Above all, Italy gave Emerson a profound and subtle experience of beauty and of his own capacity to perceive it. Beauty he knew to be indefinable, but it was to him inseparable from the sacred. In his essay, "Michael Angelo," he later wrote that beauty is best described in the Italian fashion as *"Il più nell'uno"*: "the many in one," or "multitude in unity." As such, it was not far from his concept of the universal unity of the Over-Soul: beauty was a testament to the oneness and creative center of life. Nowhere else had he been so exposed to its influence as there.

Italy gave Emerson much, and in turn deserves credit for the freedom he found there and translated not only into his "book about nature," but into his renewed, more trustful and fruitful relation with creation. It is one of the finer paradoxes of a paradoxical life that the confidence to demand that "original relation with the universe" first took root in the oldest and least forgetful country of the West.

108

~ Anatomical Theater, University of Padua. *"Heard the professor Caldania lecture upon anatomy with a subject. The form of the Lecture room was an inverted cone" with a false bottom where cadavers could be dropped to the river below should police surprise the professor.*.

~ Duomo, Milan.

~ Family of cypresses. " . . . perhaps the most satis-
factory & most valuable impressions are those which
come to each individual casually & in moments
when he is not on the hunt for wonders."

SELECTED SOURCES

The following books contribute to an understanding of Emerson's journey and its background.

Allen, Gay Wilson. *Waldo Emerson: A Biography*. New York: Viking Press, *1981*. A modern biography treating the full range of Emerson's life.

Baker, Paul. *The Fortunate Pilgrims: Americans in Italy 1800–1860*. Cambridge, Mass.: Harvard University Press, *1964*. A study of the early American students of Italian art and culture.

Barish, Evelyn. *Emerson: The Roots of Prophecy*. Princeton, N.J.: Princeton University Press, forthcoming *1989*. A critical biography focusing on Emerson's early life and thought.

Byron, George Gordon, Lord. *Childe Harold's Pilgrimage. Byron's Poetical Works*. Edited by Frederick Page. Rev. ed. Oxford: Oxford University Press, *1979*. The epic poem which Emerson knew almost by heart, written by English Romanticism's great poet.

Emerson, Ralph Waldo. *The Complete Works of Ralph Waldo Emerson*. Edited by Edward W. Emerson. *12* vols. Cambridge, Mass.: Riverside Press, *1904*.

_____. *The Letters of Ralph Waldo Emerson*. Edited by Ralph L. Rusk. *6* vols. New York: Columbia University Press, *1939*.

_____. *Journals and Miscellaneous Notebooks of Ralph Waldo Emerson*. Edited by Alfred Ferguson et al. *16* vols. Cambridge, Mass.: Harvard University Press, *1960–82*. Volume *4* is the source of all quotations not otherwise attributed in this book.

Goethe, Johann Wolfgang von. *Italian Journey: 1786–1788*. San Francisco: North Point Press, *1982*. A travel journal by the dominating genius of early Romantic thought; a model for Emerson's journey.

Highet, Gilbert. *Poets in a Landscape*. New York: Knopf, 1957. A discussion of the classical background of the literary traveler in Italy.

Montaigne, Michel de. *Montaigne's Travel Journal*. Translated and edited by Donald M. Frame. San Francisco: North Point Press, 1983. French skeptic, traveler, and Renaissance man, subject of an essay and loved by Emerson.

Novak, Barbara. *Nature and Culture: American Landscape Painting 1825–1875*. New York: Oxford University Press, 1981. Part Four illuminates American painters and writers in Italy and Europe.

Seward, Desmond, ed. *Naples: A Travellers' Companion*. New York: Atheneum, 1986. Travelers' comments about Naples from the thirteenth to the nineteenth centuries.